D1488556

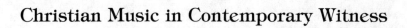

Christian Music in Contemporary Witness

CHRISTIAN MUSIC
IN CONTEMPORARY
WITNESS

Historical Antecedents and Contemporary Practices

Donald Paul Ellsworth

BAKER BOOK HOUSE
Grand Rapids, Michigan

To
JUDY
without whose love, assistance, and personal sacrifice
this book could not have been written
and to
Donald, Jr. and Geoffrey
for their patience and understanding

The completion of this book could not have been accomplished without the help of a number of individuals. I am most grateful to Dr. Donald Hustad and Dr. Phillip Landgrave for granting personal interviews. These and a number of others cordially responded to my requests for pertinent material. I must recognize the research and editorial assistance provided by my colleagues David McClain, Richard Horner, William McDonald, Dr. Rembert Carter, Dr. and Mrs. William Osborne, and my brother, Rev. Wilbur Ellsworth.

Contents

PART ONE

MUSIC FOR CHURCH OUTREACH: HISTORICAL EVIDENCE

Chapter 1

Introduction

The church's paramount responsibilities are to provide opportunities for worship, instruction, and witness. For a totally effective ministry in music, each of these three areas must be served.

Much has been written concerning the place and function of music in the service of worship. This music can be identified as formal music, such as the music of the congregation, the rehearsed, predictable music of the choir, or that which is rendered by the instrumentalists. The music of worship is directed Godward; we might, therefore, call it vertical music. It is understandable that most of the writings on church music deals primarily with the music of the church at worship, since this is the church's foremost obligation.

Significantly less has been written about the role of music in the teaching or instructional ministry of the church. This, however, is a *bona fide* part of the music ministry. Clear scriptural basis for it is given in Colossians 3:16, where Paul exhorts Christians to be "teaching and admonishing one another in psalms and hymns and spiritual songs."

Purpose and Scope of the Study

In contrast to what has been written about music in worship or instruction, even less has been written concerning church music's ministry of outreach and witness. In recent years some formal studies have been made of this unique music, but generally they have dealt with shorter, more limited periods of history.[1] No extended study has dealt specifically with the contemporary church's struggles with musical evangelism, while presenting historical perspective. Evidence shows that since the time of the early church there has been music which differs from the traditional Augustinian definition of the hymn as a "song of praise to God." This music serves a different function, and its purpose should not be confused with the music of worship. The song of testimony is directed to one's fellow man as an attempt to expose him to the New Testament gospel by means of music.

In discussing the music of evangelism, we will at times deal with expressions that are also didactic in nature and purpose. This music will be found most readily in movements and periods of religious subjectivism, and is always an attempt to find new ways to reach unchurched people in their culture. In many cases, witness music has taken on an apparently secular style in order to use musical language which the man in the marketplace can understand. To many Christians this has been, and still is, an unacceptable practice.

One of our purposes will be to show that the issue of popularized secularism in church music is not new. This historical survey of Part One proposes to show that the revolution in recent church music has important roots in history. The revolution was, however, caught up in a converging of two phenomena—an upheaval in the arts and a period of church renewal. A second purpose will be to determine whether the use of popularized church music was significantly successful in church outreach. A third purpose will be to clarify the sometimes unfortunate distinctions which exist between worship music and evangelistic music. The fourth

---

1. Several of these studies will be cited during the course of this study. Many others can be found in the bibliography.

purpose will be to present as objectively as possible the pros and cons of the use of new popular-style church music, seeking to advise today's minister of music on the most appropriate ways to achieve effective outreach.

We shall use the term *evangelism* in the broad and popular sense, to mean a deliberate effort to encourage a conversion decision and persuade to action. Evangelism may also involve an attempt to bring people from one religious system to another or from no religious commitment to church involvement.

The term *evangelism* has had various meanings in different eras and areas. At times it meant something quite different from what is generally meant today. For example, despite the length of treatment which it will receive in this study, the Reformation period probably did not see a great deal of evangelism. On the other hand, to some twentieth-century thinkers, evangelism is tantamount to the social concern and involvement of the church.[2]

The Nature of Witness Music

The form most commonly recognized in discussions of music of testimony and witness is the gospel song of the late nineteenth and early twentieth centuries. Serious church musicians have shown little interest in this form, an attitude which is often justifiable. However, the gospel song is but one example of music for witness in the total historical picture. Indeed, the different manifestations of music for evangelism transcend many periods of history. Generally these kinds of music are not considered great musical art. They are, rather, generally spontaneous and artless expressions, not necessarily created to endure, but meant to serve a purpose for a time—to urge decision and action. These songs are

---

2. This emphasis on social concern does not seem to be nearly as widespread as it once was. Recent pronouncements by groups historically considered to be "liberal" in their theology and socially inclined in their outreach, such as the National and World Councils of Churches, have placed more stress on the importance of propagating faith, and the "need for the churches to recover the ability to name the Name of Jesus Christ as Lord and Savior and to bear witness to that Name in word and deed." In "Clergy Shut Out by Laymen," *Scranton Times* (Pa.), August 31, 1970.

found growing out of movements of reformation and spiritual fervor, yet their artless, timely style usually prohibits their being considered as works of real consequence.

Erik Routley has said,

> The melodies of the revival have an easy-going quality which reflects the tendency to attract the would-be convert by offering him an idiom which will be a release from certain of his intellectual doubts and responsibilities.[3]

Evangelistic music has—indeed has had to—manifest itself differently depending on the times. Part One will point out some of the more outstanding examples of historical musical evangelism. In church music, and especially in the music of evangelism, it is not necessary for a composition to be a musical monument which can be handed down from one generation to another in order for that composition to fulfill its immediate function. As one writer has stated, "Much serviceable music dies with the generation that produced it and found it satisfying. . . . Many of the gospel hymns of the evangelistic type are a form of folklore."[4]

The evangelical church bases its code of faith and practice on Scripture. The Bible does not, however, have anything specific to say concerning music being used in evangelism. But the evangelical's practice of using music for his witness does seem to be founded on historical practice. To many in the field of musical evangelism, a major difficulty exists in the great dichotomy between music of the church and music of the marketplace. All admit that the church is to be involved in an ongoing search for new modes of expression—new styles, new sounds, new songs—in an effort to communicate with a fresh vitality the gospel's timeless message. Many feel, however, that adopting the "language of the people" constitutes a compromise of the essence of the truth of the gospel.

My interest in this subject has grown out of an observation of those who cannot see merit in any contemporary style of gospel music. But resistance to new styles of church music

---

3. Erik Routley, *The Music of Christian Hymnody*, p. 175.
4. Ilion T. Jones, *A Historical Approach to Evangelical Worship*, pp. 258–59.

and attendant tendencies toward an authoritative regulation are certainly not new to church history. As Donald Grout writes:

> There have been many instances in history of the state or some authority prohibiting certain kinds of music, acting on the principle that this matter was important to the public welfare. Music was regulated in the early constitutions of both Athens and Sparta. The writings of the Church Fathers contain many warnings against specific kinds of music. Nor is the issue dead in the 20th century. Dictatorships, both fascist and communist, have attempted to control the musical activity of their people; churches usually establish norms for the music that may be used in their services.[5]

Cycles and Trends of Church Witness

The history of church music can be traced in a number of ways. As we discuss music in evangelism, cycles or trends may be found which show the church to be in any one phase of a three-phase cycle—a period of outside persecution, a period of peace on the outside, and a period of revolution outside.[6]

Outside persecution causes the church family to seek the safety of the church and join together in a close-knit worship. When there is sufficient peace on the outside to permit an encounter between the Christian and the non-Christian outside the church, evangelism will begin. Cultural, sociological, philosophical, or artistic revolutions outside may not initially affect the church, but in many cases expressions growing out of revolution are eventually used by the Church for effective communication. These cycles in time are not of any consistent, predictable duration, but it is probable that Christian songs of witness will be more common during movements which emphasize the importance of the individual.

The church's concern for outreach has come and gone throughout its existence. The pendulum has swung toward a feeling of concern and compassion, countered thereafter by a

---

5. Donald Jay Grout, *A History of Western Music*, rev. ed., p. 9.
6. Erik Routley, *Words, Music and the Church*, p. 153.

swing toward a feeling of complacence. Then the whole cycle begins again. In every complete cycle there is a merging of the "sacra" and the "profana." Each time the church has expressed its beliefs in a contemporary way it has surged forward in evangelistic outreach, bringing scores of people into the church. And, when music of the church has been "set apart" from the laity, a new idiom generally follows to bring the two together.

The Sacred-Secular Syndrome

The identification of moral values with music and the resistance to the use of secularized music in the church are nearly as old as the church itself. Early church fathers were aware of the earlier Greek doctrine of ethos which maintained that music has distinct moral qualities and effects. Music was believed to have power to influence people along specific emotional and behavioral lines. Consequently, no innovations or foreign melodic material were admissible. It is not difficult to understand the church fathers' attitude toward the secular music of their day, since the early church existed in the midst of a largely pagan civilization.

Nevertheless, to deny that secular musical influence can be adaptable to church use is to deny the clear evidence of history. We shall see that there are examples throughout history of how music styles once considered to be hostile to church tradition have not only become compatible, but have actually lost some of the alleged defects as these styles assumed a new identity. A time of assimilation takes place when the church benefits from the influence of secular art forms.

Some of these secular sources are derived from learned art styles. Other sources, particularly those which will be studied here, are more folk-oriented in derivation and appeal. The church has borrowed the "non-churchy" ideas, styles, tunes, and rhythms in order to clothe the timeless truth of the gospel in musical language which the unchurched person will recognize and with which he can identify.

The new music which results is, then, both evangelistic and didactic, and is addressed to the people in their native tongue, not in the medieval Latin or the "language" of the church.

The intention of the church musician has been to break out from the barriers of the monastery, cathedral, or church and attempt to find new ways to reach people with the gospel.

The sacred and the secular have an influence on each other. Secular ideas and styles have originated from many sources—from the marketplace to the secular art music of the salon, concert hall, or opera house. And for centuries the following questions have been asked: Is there such a thing as "sacred music"? Is there such a thing as a "sacred" or "holy" place? How is the holy related to the material? How is God related to His world? How is the church related to secular society?

Some of these questions can be answered; others cannot. A person's responses to these questions will largely determine his position on matters of popularized witness music. We shall see that church music seems to be at its best when it does not compete with secular music, but runs parallel to it.

Friedrich Blume suggests the artificiality of categorizing musical styles as innately sacred or secular.

> The qualitative aspect of "Protestant church music" raises even more doubts. I shall not venture upon thin ice by attempting definitions, and shall confine myself to indicating how ambiguous is the division of music into "sacred," "religious," and "secular" (or half-religious and half-secular).[7]

To support the fact that there is danger in sacred-secular categorizations, Blume cites several musical examples which defy categorizing: Leonhard Lechner's *Sprüche von Leben und Tod;* Buxtehude's *Rhythmica oratorio ad unum quodlibet membrorum Christi;* Johann Rist's songs; Lasso's *Penitential Psalms;* or

> organ music from Scheidt to Reger that is not connected with a cantus firmus. . . . Is it music for the service? Music for private devotions? Music for concert performance? What about Brahms' "Deutsches Requiem" or Verdi's Requiem for Manzoni? . . . Consider the religious Singspiele that J. Theile composed for the house in the Hamburg Goose Market and

---

7. Friedrich Blume, *Protestant Church Music,* p. xiii.

the music for evening concerts that Buxtehude, organist of the Marienkirche at Lubeck, wrote for his audience of wealthy merchants. The former was intended for the opera stage, and the latter for the church gallery, yet they are as close to each other as were Bach's sacred and secular cantatas (a number of which were, in fact, identical in musical substance). Neither the contrafacta of the sixteenth century nor the parodies of the eighteenth century recognized any boundary lines of a musical nature, and in the oratorios of the nineteenth and twentieth centuries the distinctions between "sacred" and "secular" were completely erased.[8]

Should our church music ever reflect the world? Blume suggests it always does reflect the world. Are sacred and secular two distinct categories? Blume implies that they are not. Should we try to attract men to Christianity through non-Christian means? Blume further implies that it is specious to speak of music *per se* (i.e., the arrangements of pitches and durations in certain timbres) as either Christian or non-Christian. Where is the line of distinction between music that is Christian and music that is not? Blume suggests there is no such line.

The dichotomy between sacred and secular is very real for some church musicians, however. For many years, the best music has frequently been composed and performed outside the evangelical church. Some writers blame the fundamentalist churchman and the music educator for some of today's church music problems. John Lilley claims that fundamentalists are to blame for the

> awkward state of communications within the Church. The fundamentalist has urged his people to withdraw from "worldliness," while the educator has thoroughly compartmentalized the study of music so that it fails to have a meaning in a total sense.[9]

In this century, the evangelical church has passed through a period in which there was a strict compartmentalization of

---

8. Ibid.

9. John M. Lilley, "New Principles of Worship Based on Multi-Media Experience in Corporate Worship," p. 17.

music styles. This attitude is breaking down today, as it has in previous times. Modern man hears a great amount of music through the media of radio, television, and recordings, and today's Christian is not so often offended at these "secular" styles when heard in the world. We are now living in the part of the cycle where much of the idea of the sacred versus the secular has modified.

As early as 1939, Warren Allen said,

> Leading historians are no longer so sure of strict and narrow classifications of "sacred" and "secular," the "good" vs. the "popular"; we are getting away from attempts to distinguish "superior" from "inferior" phrases of musical art in an evolutionary series. This means no abandonment of a belief in standards, however; on the contrary, appreciation of music will be on a higher plane when we learn to recognize sincerity in musical art, regardless of classification, function, or epoch.[10]

This book will deal with the specific phenomena of popularized music for witness, and will provide historic evidence of a "contemporization" of church music for communicating the gospel in relevant musical "language."

Summary of Historical Evidence

Church musicians realize that there have been great changes in the musical forms of the church throughout history. Not all of these changes have been rooted in the church itself. In any period of spiritual revival the old "churchy" symbols lose their meaning and newer ones are sought. Generally these new styles, forms, or symbols will be discovered outside the church.

The idea of borrowing from outside the orthodox church had its start in the early years of Christianity when the church practiced antiphonal singing as a countering device to the early heresies. Popular sacred folk tunes and carols were sung in the Middle Ages, as were the *laudi spirituali, cantigas,* macaronic hymns, and various *contrafacta.* All of these

---

10. Warren Dwight Allen, *Philosophies of Music History,* p. 146.

existed and even prospered for a time without the sanction of the church; in most cases, however, each phenomenon was a result of spiritual revival. The recent revolution in church music is not, then, without historical precedent.

The evangelical church has always believed in outreach, evangelism, and missionary service. In most evangelical church meetings, the pastor "preaches for a decision." Evangelicals believe that the Holy Spirit periodically blesses the church with a special season of revival. In some cases an individual may be used to initiate revival of religious fervor. Paul, Augustine, Savanarola, Luther, Calvin, the Wesleys, Moody, Billy Sunday, and Billy Graham are some who have contributed to religious awakenings. All of these revivals had their special outpouring of inspired Christian song.

For a time these new styles of secularized church music result in chaos within the church. We have gone through such a period in the sixties with the advent of sacred pop and folk styles. As was pointed out earlier, the musical and textual material in most of the music of witness hinders its ability to endure. This was one of the major difficulties with evangelical church music of the 1930s to the 1960s. The idiom was created in the nineteenth century, and was perpetuated in the twentieth by many gospel composers who had less ability and taste than their musical predecessors.

An answer to the problem of locating new and meaningful witness music came from Great Britain through a strong evangelical youth movement in the 1950s. This popular-style church music quickly found its way to America, where, as in England, there was an almost complete capitulation to folk and rock music styles. Evangelical musicians soon teamed with music publishers to create one of the most revolutionary and divisive periods in the history of church music. But this chaos, as well as many other earlier chaotic periods of church renewal, came largely as a result of a search for a language for witness and for expressions of Christian experience.

Disorders of this kind have usually resulted in order and maturity in musical writing. When gross transplant from the marketplace begins to wane, and more maturity is evident, the new idioms are accepted by the church. The secular influence remains, however, and music created for outreach begins to find its way into the service of worship. In time, many of the once-offensive rhythms, harmonies, texts, and instruments are made more subtle or disguised in choir anthems, instrumental solos, or vocal solos.

Organization of the Study

This book is in two major parts. Part One (chaps. 1–6) is a brief historical survey of music for church outreach from the time of the early church until 1960. To understand any religious or cultural phenomenon one must be familiar with its historical setting, its tradition, and the issues involved. Part Two (chaps. 7–10) deals with the major issues caused by the music of church witness since 1960.

Chapter 2

Witness Music of the Early Church and Middle Ages

The Meaning of Witness Music in the Early Church

For the first thousand years of the Christian church, its music was primarily controlled by the needs of corporate worship. The best music was that which conformed to the church's discipline and submitted to church regulation. During much of this first millenium, although sacred and secular art frequently moved in the same direction, the concepts of sacred and secular were quite distinct. Even secular art was usually controlled by the church and its artists.

Secular music existed before the sacred music of the early church, however, and when the two began their parallel existence, the relationship was not always cordial. For the first three hundred years, the church was an unsanctioned organization within the Roman Empire; early church leaders felt that the church could not afford to involve itself with a pagan society. The world disliked the church; by the same token, the church frequently had to resist the world's values.

Music in the early church could be termed "evangelistic" only as it functioned to extend doctrinal teaching. There is evidence of this didactic use of music throughout most of church history, but such activity increased during those periods when the orthodox church was threatened by heretical teachings and movements.

Description of Early Church Music

The clearest biblical injunction for musical witness, both in the early church and later, is found in two parallel passages in the New Testament referring to the "spiritual song" (Eph. 5:19 and Col. 3:16). Some writers believe this was the musical equivalent of "speaking with tongues."[1] Many church musicians and historians agree that it was likely a kind of improvised folk song, apparently limited to those who were "spirit-filled." The Holy Spirit was the source of that supernatural musical expression which was a gift to the early Christian community. The spiritual song was possibly an ecstatic, improvised musical utterance. As Richard Eastcott has written,

> Music, in the early ages of christianity [*sic*], is said to have drawn the Gentiles into the church through novelty, and we are told that they were so captivated, and liked its ceremonies so well, that many of them were baptized before they left the congregation.[2]

There is at least one scriptural reference to a group of presumably non-Christians giving attention to the singing of early Christians (Acts 16:25). It is possible that this rapturous singing was typical of the early church. It may have been involved in what Donald Grout calls "the creation of hymns under the inspiration of strong religious feeling, somewhat the way today new phrases of text and new melodic variations spontaneously arise during the enthusiasm of a revival meeting or folk song."[3]

---

1. Erik Routley, *Music Leadership in the Church*, p. 89.

2. Elwyn Wienandt, citing Richard Eastcott's "Sketches on the Origin, Progress and Effects of Music" (1793), in *Opinions on Church Music*, p. 97.

3. Grout, *History of Western Music*, p. 19.

Ralph Martin supports this practice by quoting A. B. MacDonald as he writes of the early Christian church:

> "We should expect that a movement which released so much emotion, and loyalty, and enthusiasm, would find expression in Song." After quoting cases of religious awakening in the history of the Church in later years (such as the eighteenth century Revival) and showing that these have been accompanied by outbursts of song, he goes on: "So it would have been strange indeed if the Church had remained songless in that first glorious dawn when the light of Christ came breaking across the horizons, making all things new."
> But Christian song did not break forth upon a world which had been hitherto dumb and in which hymns were unknown. The Church . . . borrowed many of its forms of worship from the Temple and synagogue.[4]

The apostle Paul knew the value of religious song. Although we cannot be certain just what he and Silas sang that night in the jail at Philippi, no doubt they sang in an attempt to bring comfort and encouragement to each other. One result of their singing is clearly recorded. The jailor asked, "Sirs, what must I do to be saved?" (Acts 16:30). Unquestionably the jailor was moved to ask this question partly because of the great earthquake which they had just experienced. However, there is nothing intrinsic in an earthquake which would encourage a man to seek to be saved. Paul's and Silas's singing must have had something to do with it. We can be reasonably sure that the songs were at least meaningful to those prisoners who were listening, because Paul writes elsewhere (I Cor. 14:15) that singing is to be done with the understanding. When Paul sang, it was very likely that he used musical parts of the services of the temple and synagogue as well as simple hymns of Christian origin which were beginning to appear among the apostles and disciples.

The synagogue, which apparently sprang up during the exile, was even more important than the temple in the days of Christ and the apostles. By the time Christ was ready to begin His public ministry, synagogues were found in most cities of the Holy Land. Every such place stood for public worship and

---

4. Ralph P. Martin, *Worship in the Early Church,* p. 40.

teaching. The synagogue, then, was the natural place to begin the evangelization of any community. Christ and the apostles on occasion used the synagogues, and the early church incorporated many of the synagogical forms in their gatherings. In this setting, the scriptural expositions of the preachers were largely didactic, not rhetorical. The fountainhead of their evangelism and mission of outreach was public worship.[5]

We do not have much information regarding early church evangelism. That public and private witness did take place, however, is certain from the evidence recorded in the Book of Acts (8:5; 17:18). But we cannot be certain of the results, according to Michael Green:

> It is not possible to assess realistically the extent to which the evangelism conducted by the early church was successful. For one thing, we have no means of comparing their "successes" with their "failures."
>
> Nor is it possible to read off from a study of evangelism in antiquity the answers to our contemporary problems in communicating the gospel. However, some aspects of their approach stand out significantly, and are important for the Church to take heed of in any age.[6]

Upon conversion, the early Christians used every means in their power to share their discovery with others. House meetings, informal conversations, open-air preaching, addresses in church and synagogue, arguments in the marketplace and philosophical school, social visits, personal testimony, and letter-writing were all used to further their supreme aim. Since they were singing Christians as well, it seems reasonable to believe that music was a useful means of communication in some of these areas of witness. As Green says, "When men have the will to speak of their Lord, they find no shortage of ways in which to do it."[7]

Evangelism today is often associated with mass meetings. The early church rarely used this method, since large-scale Christian gatherings were banned by imperial edict until A.D.

---

5. Andrew W. Blackwood, *The Fine Art of Public Worship,* pp. 40–41.

6. Michael Green, *Evangelism in the Early Church,* p. 274.

7. Ibid., p. 278.

313, when the church became a tolerated institution. Very soon thereafter it began to be a unified force. In its first three hundred years, however, the church's most important evangelistic endeavors were carried on in the home and on a personal, private basis. In the more public meetings, attractive means were utilized in order to draw the crowds and hold them. If some visual aid were available, it was usually used.[8] In these open-air meetings, teaching and evangelism went hand in hand. The example for this may have been taken from Paul, "who took over the lecture hall of Tyrannus when he was staying for his three years in Ephesus. This was a most impressive piece of Christian opportunism."[9]

The people of the early church preached and taught for a variety of purposes. At times it was to relate the events of the gospel (the story of Christ's ministry, death, burial, and resurrection) in an effort to convince their hearers that Jesus is the Messiah. The speakers sometimes told the meaning of these events, and at other times they tried to persuade the people to act upon the significance of these events.

Statements by Early Church Historians

Although there is still speculation concerning the nature of the songs of the early church, it seems safe to assume that the melodies were rooted in the folk tradition of the time. As Donald Grout has said,

> It is likely that some of the hymns of the early Church were sung to what would now be called folk melodies, and it is possible that some of these melodies eventually found their way into the official chant repertoire.[10]

About A.D. 112, Pliny the Younger recorded that the Christians in Asia Minor sang "songs to Christ as a god."[11] Also, one Niceta of Remesiana was instrumental in spreading

---

8. Ibid., p. 205.

9. Ibid.

10. Grout, *History of Western Music,* p. 13.

11. Constantine E. Pritchard and Edward R. Bernard, eds., *Selected Letters of Pliny,* p. 124.

the gospel among fourth-century pagans in southeastern Europe, largely by his singing "sweet songs of the cross."[12] We can also be quite certain that many of these tunes were taken from popular secular sources.[13]

What we know of the mainstream of the first six centuries of church music is essentially limited to what has been recorded. The records deal mostly with liturgical music, and not all sacred music. We can assume that people sang outside the church, both purely secular and non-liturgical sacred music, but we have no record of these songs. What information we do have about non-liturgical music or secular music comes from sources which treat it incidentally or with hostility.

The music of the early church was most likely unmetrical plainsong, whereas secular music was probably metrical and dance-like. During the first centuries the church continually borrowed secular musical sources and practices. It is likely, moreover, that the secular world also borrowed from the church.

The Use of Music to Refute Heresy

Many early church leaders harbored strong feelings against using anything except the Psalms for their singing.[14] The spreading of heresy through musical means served to strengthen their cautious attitude. In the fourth century and after, Arianism (a denial of the deity of Christ) was the dominant heresy. Despite official condemnation, Arianism continued to flourish. Even Chrysostom, with all his oratoric ability, could not stem the tide. The Arians made it a regular practice on Saturdays, Sundays, and festival days to march through the streets singing their hymns. Then Chrysostom,

---

12. Albert E. Bailey, *The Gospel in Hymns: Backgrounds and Interpretations*, p. 214.

13. Grout, *History of Western Music*, p. 18.

14. A very strong case in support of this position is presented by John McNaugher and others in the book, *The Psalms in Worship*. The authors go so far as to claim that even the New Testament reference to "psalms, hymns and spiritual songs" is actually speaking of nothing more than different types of Psalms.

by using some of the Arians' techniques, began to win the upper hand in influencing the population. So it became clear that sacred singing could be used for good as well as for ill.

Edward Ninde writes,

> With the financial aid of the Empress Eudoxia, he [Chryso-stom] organized splendid processions of the orthodox party, and they went forth carrying torches and crosses, and singing with imperial pomp the hymns of Christ. Often, gathered in the church porticoes "glowing with the processional torches," they would spend the long, quiet hours of the night in song. Not only was the enemy put to shame, but it led to a much freer use of hymns in the church services, both by day and at night.[15]

We can discover, therefore, as early as the fourth century, precedents for the evangelistic street meetings which have been used in recent years by evangelistic groups such as the Salvation Army. Eventually the public singing of Arian hymns was suppressed by imperial edict, and the singing of orthodox hymns in the churches became a regular practice.

In citing early Christian examples of popularized sacred music, we must consider the work of Ephraem Syrus (c. 306–c. 373), a monk of the ancient city of Edena in Meso-potamia. Apparently Christianity flourished in this city until late in the second century, when a teacher by the name of Bardesanes (154–222) became prominent. Although he claimed to be a Christian, his teachings were filled with gnos-tic heresy. To make matters worse, he popularized his views through poems and music, frequently putting his accounts into hymnic forms and setting them to popular tunes. Ac-cording to the *Harvard Dictionary,* "Bardesanes and his son (or disciple?) Harmonius wrote a complete Gnostic Psalter, a collection of poetic paraphrases of the Psalms. Its great popu-lar success led to imitations among the Christians."[16] These new forms appealed to the public immediately. Adults and

---

15. Edward S. Ninde, *Nineteen Centuries of Christian Song*, p. 24.

16. Willi Apel, "Hymn," in *Harvard Dictionary of Music*, second ed., p. 397.

children sang the songs, spreading gnostic philosophies at work and play.

Bardesanes was dead when Ephraem came to Edena, but Bardesanes' teachings had made strong inroads into the traditional faith. In what must have been one of the first examples (but certainly not the last) of such a practice, Ephraem began to attack the heretical enemy with its own methods. He wrote hymns of orthodox doctrine, adopting tunes which were already popular with the people, even using some that Bardesanes had composed. As Ninde writes,

> He organized and personally trained choirs of young women to sing his hymns in proper form, and they led in choruses on Sundays and feast days. The result was that the whole city was stirred, crowds came to the orthodox services and heresy was driven from the field. Ephraem's writings are little known today, but he is remembered as one who put the musical service on a popular basis.[17]

Another musical device used in the early church was antiphonal singing.[18] The first known example of antiphony in the church was at Antioch, Syria, early in the fourth century, and consequently, this city is frequently regarded as the birthplace of Christian song. One of the purposes of antiphonal singing was to attract people to the orthodox congregations and to counter the current heresies. The antiphonal and responsorial chanting of hymns was an effective means for attracting and evangelizing people, even if the practice was not conceived by the orthodox Christian church. Gustave Reese discusses this use of antiphony:

> The ascetics Flavian and Diodoros are credited with having introduced it into the orthodox Christian practice of Antioch in the 4th century when, to combat the Arian heresy, they sought to make the services more attractive by assigning the chanting of the psalm-verses to the congregation. Its members were divided into two semi-choruses, one of men, one of

---

17. Ninde, *Nineteen Centuries of Christian Song*, p. 21.

18. References to antiphonal singing are to be found in various sources, including Tertullian. See Tertullian, *De Oratione* 27 (*Patrologia Latina* I.1194); *De Anima* 9 (*Patrologia Latina* II.660).

women and children, and the groups alternated with one another in the singing of the psalm-verses and combined in singing an Alleluia or, perhaps, some new refrain. The intercalating of passages of song between psalm-verses became, in the course of time, an organized practice and was destined to be imitated with telling effect in the West.[19]

Because hymn singing was such an effective means of Christian witness, it is reasonable to assume that the same was true of antiphonal singing, since the two practices were so closely related. As Louis Benson has written:

What was new at Milan, apart from the antiphonal singing Ambrose brought over from the East, was the hymns themselves. The assembly, the fervor, the hymnody of edification, were apostolic,—the hymns were Ambrosian.[20]

Basil the Great (c. 329–379) wrote of the persuasive effects of certain kinds of music, suggesting that they helped people to "swallow" Christian teaching, "just as wise physicians who, when giving the fastidious rather bitter drugs to drink, frequently smear the cup with honey."[21] Later in this same homily, Basil reported on the popularity and effectiveness of early Christian singing:

For, never has any one of the many indifferent persons gone away easily holding in mind either an apostolic or prophetic message, but they do chant the words of the psalms, even in the home, and they spread them around in the market place.[22]

One of the most imposing figures in church history is Ambrose (c. 340–397), Bishop of Milan. His priestly apprenticeship was in Syria, where he became familiar with the Syrian practices of antiphony and hymn singing. When he was moved to Milan he brought with him many of the traditions to which he had been exposed in Syria, and he used some of them to fight the Arian controversy and to improve the ser-

---

19. Gustave Reese, *Music in the Middle Ages*, p. 68.
20. Louis F. Benson, *The Hymnody of the Christian Church*, p. 69.
21. Saint Basil, *Exegetic Homilies*, trans. Sister Agnes Clare Way, p. 152.
22. Ibid.

vices in his cathedral. In this way, Ambrose was responsible for the introduction of antiphony and hymn singing in the Occident. Hymns and sacred songs were borrowed from earlier times and some were newly composed, giving a boost to the popularizing of sacred song. The Ambrosian syllabic settings often were similar to the street dances of the day.

Hilary (c. 315–367), bishop of the ancient city of Poitiers in Gaul, is said to have been one of the first Latin hymnists. But more important than what he wrote is the reason he wrote it—to counter heresy. The Arian heresy was now in full bloom; even the emperor had been influenced by it. Hilary was one of Arianism's bitterest enemies, and he denounced the emperor as the Antichrist. For this he was banished to Phrygia. But even in Phrygia, Hilary found Arianism, and he found the people in and out of the church singing songs expressing these religious beliefs. Later, his exile ended, he returned home with the idea, like Ephraem and Chrysostom before him, of the good use of Christian song in combating false doctrine. Immediately he began composing hymns and preparing hymnbooks for his diocese.

With the exception of Augustine's *De Musica,* a complex synthesis of music theory and theology, all of the references to music in the writings of the early church fathers fall into three groups: (1) descriptions of early musical use; (2) praises of music; and (3) protests against musical abuse.[23] The writings and decisions of the patristic church show a keen awareness of the power of music and a desire to guard Christians against music that would damage their faith. Some of the church fathers revealed more theological expertise than a knowledge of musical principles, relying to a large degree on the system of Greek moralism. Their problem was much the same as Christian musical leaders of any age—to justify the natural principles of musical science with what they considered to be the supernatural revealings of doctrinal and moral principles. Despite the tenuousness of some of their positions and principles, the advice of the early church fathers was generally very effective.

---

23. Erik Routley, *The Church and Music,* p. 45.

The Secularization and Popularization
of Church Music in the Middle Ages

The medieval period saw much integration of secular and sacred art and music.[24] At the same time music was held in a position of high honor in the church. To devout Christians, music was an important part of religious life. In his writings on medieval liberal arts, Boethius reestablished the classical connection between music and human morals which continued throughout the Middle Ages. In addition, popular music derived much of its style and form from the music of the church. The emphasis was upon simple tunes, and repetition which made the songs easy to remember, as well as attractive, to both singer and listener. Since there was a great deal of exchange between the sacred and secular, it is frequently difficult to distinguish between the secular, popular songs and the non-liturgical sacred songs of the more aggressive religious movements.

The Mass and motet of the later Middle Ages sometimes used the music of popular song in the church.[25] In the Masses the *cantus firmi* were often borrowed secular tunes, frequently so altered that they were scarcely recognizable. The composer needed just as much skill to compose with a borrowed melody as he needed to create an original one. He experienced little difficulty in borrowing from outside the church for two reasons. First, the same musicians were writing both secular and sacred music, an indication that these two idioms were similar. Second, despite great similarity, the tunes were generally camouflaged through the skills of the composer.

Tropes and Sequences

Probably the most important development in the evolution of Christian chant from the ninth to the twelfth centuries is the *trope*. In the eighth or ninth centuries florid melodies, or

---

24. Reese, *Music in the Middle Ages,* pp. 201, 218.
25. Ibid., pp. 357–58, 421.

tropes, were added to sections of the chant that seemed to invite such treatment—such as the Alleluia. These additions were attached to the beginning, end, or sometimes between certain parts of a liturgical melody. Singers, eventually finding the *melismas* difficult to memorize, added a text, one syllable per note. Gustave Reese writes,

> The practice of thus applying text spread rapidly, especially in the monasteries, and eventually many parts of the established liturgy were interlarded with new melodies set to new words which enlarged upon the sentiments expressed in the passages embellished.[26]

One kind of trope, the *sequence,* most clearly evolved into a definite form. In the sequence, long melodies were attached to the *jubilus* (the final "a" of "Alleluia") and were separated into shorter strophes to permit the singers to breathe. In performance, each strophe was repeated. In time, words were added to some of the strophes, "producing pairs of lines of parallel or approximately parallel structure whenever the words were added to both a strophe and its repetition."[27] A collection of melodies resulted that were without words or with words under only parts of the melody.

Sequences soon became very popular and spread into all of Western Europe. Many of the familiar melodies were provided with new texts, some of them in the vernacular. Gustave Reese points out that the eleventh-century sequence "Laetabundus" became a model for over a hundred imitations.[28] Sequences became so popular that they threatened the liturgy, but the Council of Trent (1545–63) banned all but four of them after some of the sequences had made their way into the Mass. Because of the syllabic nature of the sequence, it was the most folk-like of all the chant styles, making it a veritable religious folk song in the vernacular.

---

26. Ibid., pp. 185–86.
27. Ibid., p. 187.
28. Ibid., p. 189.

Macaronic Hymns and Contrafacta

Other examples of the popularization of church language in the Middle Ages include the use of macaronic hymns and *contrafacta*. The macaronic hymns were of mixed language, with some lines in Latin and some in the vernacular. The contrafacted hymns were as extensive as they were important. They were created by combining an already popular melody with a new text. The popular tunes were useful in disseminating new doctrine and in activating the congregation to service. These sacred parodies of secular songs were written in the thirteenth century by composers such as Heinrich von Laufenberg and others. Many of the songs were used in the church throughout the Middle Ages—and even on into the Renaissance—though not officially admitted to the liturgy. Some of the songs were used by the Roman Catholic church and also by the Reformers. According to Reese, these songs were those

> in which the melodies of the old pieces were retained, but the texts rewritten to suit Protestant ideas—in short, *contrafacta*. As earlier, the distinction between secular and sacred music was so vague in the first decades of the Reformation that no hesitation was felt in adapting sacred texts to secular melodies, just as the Catholics did not hesitate to write Masses based on secular tunes.[29]

Secular Song Style

Because secular songs of the Middle Ages did not enjoy the care and protection which the church's music did, much of it was not preserved. In the oral tradition, lay singers could feel free to change tunes, perhaps even taking pride in their own elaborations. It has been impossible, therefore, to restore the oldest melodies with accuracy, particularly since so many of them have survived in staffless neume notation. In many cases it is difficult to distinguish between a church style and a lay style. It must be noted that "secular" may simply

---

29. Gustave Reese, *Music in the Renaissance,* pp. 674–75.

mean non-liturgical, religious songs in the vernacular. It was natural and easy for singers like the troubadours, trouvères, and Minnesingers to model their songs on the ecclesiastical melodies which they frequently heard in the churches. The lay composer did not find it incongruous to adapt a love poem to a liturgical melody. Many "secular" songs had religious subjects. Even in song texts it is sometimes difficult to discern the origin or function since many of the early extra-church songs were in Latin, the language of the church.

Laudi spirituali and Gesslerlieder

Through such strong traditions as the *Laudi spirituali* and *Geisslerlieder* in the thirteenth and fourteenth centuries, we have evidence that the enthusiastic underworld of religious activity was influential in the spread of popular sacred songs. These songs have a relationship to more modern revival songs in that all of them shared a strophic form and simple melody. The *Laudi,* which continued into the eighteenth century, were non-liturgical songs of devotion and praise sung in the vernacular. These songs became very popular with the people. The earliest *Laudi* appear to have started with the flagellants of northern Italy in the mid-thirteenth century. The songs were sung at public meetings and took their musical examples from the popular, secular songs of the day.

The flagellanti, so called because they preached and practiced self-scourging, had a strong influence in the secularization of spiritual music in the thirteenth and fourteenth centuries, and are responsible for both the *Laudi spirituali* and the *Geisslerlieder.* They were particularly active in the mid-fourteenth century when the Black Death was rampant throughout Europe. As Edward Ninde writes,

> They wandered from town to town, their half-naked bodies streaked with blood, chanting weird hymns and in frenzied passion summoning the multitudes to repentance.[30]

---

30. Ninde, *Nineteen Centuries of Christian Song,* p. 55.

In the mid-fourteenth century a tradition of popular religious hymnody appeared among a German sect of flagellants known as *Geissler,* also very common following the Black Death. Some of the *Geisslerlieder* show a resemblance to some of the later chorale forms.[31]

Another thirteenth-century musical form was the *cantiga,* a Spanish monophonic song, usually in honor of the Virgin Mary. An earlier type of great interest is the *cantiga d'amigo,* of c. 1200, the song of a girl in love.[32] Here is another example of secular form finding a place in sacred music.[33]

The Medieval Carol

In addition to medieval liturgical hymns sung only by the clergy or choir, there was much private use of religious poetry in the vernacular. Important examples were the carols and other types of semi-religious songs, popular not only at Christmastime, but also on Easter and other special days as well. English carols date from the fifteenth century, but carols were known in France as early as the thirteenth century. Written in a folk idiom, carols were popular religious songs designed for devotional use outside of the church. They were not liturgical, nor were they initially allowed in the church.

The dominant tone of the medieval carol was one of happiness and joy. Even when the song was about Christ's crucifixion, the mood created was one of victory and rejoicing. In later years the carol influence did find its way into the orthodox worship of the church. Contemporary hymns could also benefit by borrowing some of the secular flavor of the carols for the cause of musical evangelism.

Speaking of the carol, Routley has said,

> A return to the carol in our public praise is a first step to good hymn writing. . . .
> Consider again how the ballad carols juxtaposed theological

---

31. Cf. Reese, *Music in the Middle Ages,* p. 239.
32. Apel, "Cantigua," in *Harvard Dictionary of Music,* p. 129.
33. Cf. Reese, *Music in the Middle Ages,* pp. 244–48.

ideas which seem incompatible to the modern mind. Especially did they juxtapose the passion and laughter, redemption and the *dance,* atonement and a *love song.* It was the special genius of those ancient ages to make those bold collocations of ideas which Protestantism normally separates.[34]

In the later Middle Ages, the carol helped bridge the gap between the sacred and the secular when semi-secular words were given doctrinal and theological associations and then sung to ballad tunes.[35]

Medieval Sacred Theater

With a few notable exceptions nearly everyone in medieval Europe was at least nominally Christian and therefore few felt the need for evangelism. Since so many members of church congregations were illiterate, however, a most effective practice was instituted by the church: the creation of visual aids to teach Bible stories and spiritual principles. In this way the Bible was made to live for the people. Some of the more common means included the use of stained glass windows and statues for visual aids, and church plays which were performed either on the porch of a church or taken "on the road" in wagons—not unlike a modern carnival or circus.

The "liturgical dramas," an outgrowth of troping (see p. 36), could more accurately be called "ecclesiastical dramas." The earliest dramas appeared in tropes to Introits for Christmas and Easter. As Reese explains, "The freedom with which medieval artists added both text and music to the established liturgy developed naturally to the point where tropes with dramatic content were actually dramatized."[36] These plays used music from a variety of sources: antiphons, sequences, church hymns, "sacra" and "profana" secular music, and newly composed tunes. We have no solid evidence that these plays were given for evangelistic purposes, but we do know

---

34. Erik Routley, *Hymns Today and Tomorrow,* p. 165.

35. For additional information on the carol, see Erik Routley, *The English Carol.*

36. Reese, *Music in the Middle Ages,* p. 194.

that they reminded the people of the important principles of their faith.

In discussing sacred drama, Alan Rich states,

> As long ago as 1000 A.D., the church itself was often used by groups of actors and singers for the reenactment of Biblical stories, and the entertainments were often rather raucous. In medieval France and Italy, these entertainments occurred regularly. There would be jugglers and acrobats, dancers dressed in lurid costumes, sometimes with animal heads, performing the most hilarious and farfetched parodies of some of the most beloved stories from both Old and New Testaments. Church fathers, then too, were often horrified, but they also recognized the value of these entertainments. It was a way, after all, of dramatizing the message of God for a crowd that was often unable to read the Bible (or anything else) for itself.[37]

Some of the medieval religious dramas have survived. One of the most famous, the "Play of Daniel," was created in the twelfth or early thirteenth century by students at the Abbey of Beauvais. It relates the two most famous episodes of the prophet Daniel, the translation of the handwriting on the wall during Belshazzar's feast, and the casting of Daniel into the lion's den.[38]

Rich continues,

> The most striking thing about "Daniel" is that, for all its religiosity of theme, it is a lively show, full of dancing and colorful effects. Compared to the complex, austere music that was being created for actual church services at the time, it is a joyous romp. The melodies are a great deal like the popular music of the time, and a range of instruments was used in it that enhanced greatly the color and rhythm of the music itself. In other words, "Daniel" represents the Word of God turned into a popular entertainment, using the popular idiom of the time.[39]

---

37. Alan Rich, "Religion With a Rock Beat," pp. 17–19.

38. After careful editing for modern performance, by Noah Greenberg, director, this drama was recorded by the New York Pro Musica.

39. Rich, "Religion With a Rock Beat," pp. 17–19.

Rich maintains that today's sacred musicals are a latter-day manifestation of a phenomenon which has been part of the Christian church for centuries. Indeed, church-related drama has seen a rebirth in the last decade, not only within the church as an aid to worship, but also outside the church as a force for Christian witness.

It is important to note that there are historical examples of the arts being used outside the church for purposes of teaching and witness for the faith. Unfortunately, though music for such use within the church is easily cited, sacred music for use outside the church has been less often documented and even less frequently written down and collected. Nevertheless, it is known to have existed in various forms. Even in the medieval church, sacred music was used both in the church and outside of it, not only for teaching, but also for evangelistic outreach.

After the liturgical dramas came the mystery plays, which were popular from the fourteenth to the sixteenth centuries. These mysteries came under secular sponsorship and used the vernacular. They were dramatic representations based on biblical subjects, elaborately staged and in some instances continued for periods of twenty days or longer. They used music only incidentally—for processionals, fanfares, and dances—occasionally including plainsong, folk songs, and everyday songs of the people.[40] Here again is evidence of the use of secular tunes with a sacred theme for the spiritual instruction of the people. The mysteries were not designed for the liturgy, but they did deal with themes from the Bible. In essence, they were the major instructional tool for the lay people of the church. The content of the mysteries helped educate the layman in church doctrine, while the more popular musical idiom helped engage his interest on a more personal level. This combination again illustrates the secularization occurring in the Middle Ages.[41]

---

40. *Harvard Dictionary of Music*, p. 487.

41. For more information on recent interest in church drama, see Harold A. Daugherty, "A Study of John La Montaine's Trilogy of Pageant-Operas for Christmas," pp. 7–11, 13–15. Also see B. Howard Stevenson, "Everyman: A Creative Experiment in Church Music Drama," Introduction.

The Bohemian Hussites

During the Middle Ages, congregational singing was practically unknown except in certain splinter sects. It was largely with the Bohemian Brethren, the followers of John Hus (c. 1369–1415), that we see the opportunity to sing restored to the congregation. Hus believed that the people had the right to share in the church's song, and he and his followers wrote many hymns for use in their religious gatherings. He preached the gospel from the pulpit, but he also used the hymns as homilies. This is a significant example of the direct use of congregational song for the purpose of telling the gospel, not just from the clergy to the people, but also from person to person through the unified singing of hymns. In this we have an example of music used in the church service in order that the congregation might better understand the gospel of Christ. This is true musical evangelism.

Like the Hussites, other pre-Reformation, schismatic groups were singing songs of their own. These were religious songs of great evangelical intensity, set to tunes of the secular, dance-like kind used by the common people. Concerning this, and looking toward the Reformation, Routley says,

> The old assumptions about the church musician are going to come under heavy fire, and some of them are going to disappear for good. The secret of this historically is that the Reformation itself was a product of the same forces which produced the great outbreak of art and philosophy at the end of the Middle Ages. It is no coincidence that the founders of modern Protestantism came on the scene just when the church music had fully "found itself."[42]

Conclusion

Church music at the end of the Middle Ages was strongly influenced by secular forms, and within some of the schismatic sects, congregational participation was on the increase. It is now clear that the stage was being set for the days of the Reformation and its great use of hymns by the laity as well as

42. Routley, *Music Leadership in the Church*, p. 22.

the clergy. Taking its cue from the secularization of sacred songs in the Middle Ages, the Reformation built upon the basic principle that the sacred and secular idioms could be combined in church music with no real hindrance to the content and message of the song. The leaders of the Reformation would have done well to develop further the ideas set forth in the Middle Ages. From samples of medieval non-liturgical sacred music, it appears that much secularization and popularization had taken place and that there was developing a merger of the styles which were so often separated into sacred and secular.

Chapter 3

Witness Music
of the Sixteenth
and Seventeenth Centuries

The Sixteenth Century:
Martin Luther

By the time of the Reformation, interplay between sacred and secular musical forms was commonplace. However, there was much tension between theological demands and musical trends of the day. Before the Reformation there had been evangelical leaders who believed in the spiritual efficacy of congregational hymn singing. But it was the reappearance of the popular hymn espoused by Martin Luther (1483–1546) that signaled a return of worship music to the populace. Luther's hymns also became devices for the "propagation of the faith, and great masses of people with his melodies on their lips sang themselves into the stream of the Protestant Reformation."[1]

It must be emphasized that there was music both for worship and for evangelism. Until the time of Luther, most of the non-liturgical music was for use outside the church; with the

---

1. George W. Stansbury, "The Music of the Billy Graham Crusades," p. 10.

Reformation, some of this music was brought into the church for purposes of worship. Whereas most of the secularized music of the Middle Ages was devotional or didactic, the music of the early sixteenth century was intended more to edify believers or attract non-believers. The trend of church music during the Reformation was toward congregational participation and spreading the gospel.

The Lutherans were able to build on a great heritage of popular religious music which had originated in the Middle Ages.[2] Luther felt that the hymns and the idea of hymn singing would attract a congregation. Luther, himself a musician and poet, brought to his Reformation activities a wide, rich variety of musical styles. He loved the German folk song, and was well acquainted with the music of the Roman Church. However, he relied on congregational songs in the vernacular to spread effectively the doctrinal views of the Reformation.[3] In the large, urban churches Luther continued to use Latin, but in the smaller, rural parishes the vernacular was more effective. Often he compromised by using macaronic hymns (bilingual, Latin-German, non-liturgical hymns) as well as the *Laudi spirituali*. Luther also found great use for *Leisen* texts (sacred songs of the Minnesinger and Meistersinger) and folk hymns written in a style the people could recognize. This borrowing indicates that a significant amount of popular, semi-sacred German songs were available for ready and extensive use by Luther and other Reformers.[4]

Luther was quick to see what a help sacred song could be. By getting the people to sing their religious beliefs, and by providing songs and instruction for improving their singing, he facilitated the whole process of reformation. According to Warren Allen, "There is evidence, therefore, for his [Luther's] interest in music education and in the general Lutheran tendency to simplify and popularize the music of the church."[5] Luther had the good sense to reject very little, whether words or music, even from the Roman church. He acted

---

2. Blume, *Protestant Church Music*, p. 19.
3. Ibid., p. 13.
4. Blume, *Protestant Church Music*, p. 30.
5. Allen, *Philosophies of Music History*, p. 6.

as a purifier, not a destroyer. His concern for reaching both the educated and the uneducated of his day made him willing to combine the sacred and the secular for music designed to communicate to the people. That "God preaches the gospel through music"[6] was evident to all who were willing to listen and understand. Luther saw no reason why so many good tunes could not be used by the church, and freely borrowed melodies from many different places. Sacred words were added to the music of the popular ballads of the day.

The secular origins of many of the Lutheran tunes are easy to identify. Luther himself borrowed the melody of "Wach auf, wach auf, du Schöne" ("Wake up, wake up, thou lovely one") and substituted his own words, "Nun freut euch, lieben Christen g'mein" ("Now be joyful, dear Christians"). Other chorale lyricists used or adopted melodies of earlier religious folk songs (e.g., *Leisen*), which also had secular origins. Some of the chorale tunes most likely had plainsong roots, and some were completely original, but they were all finally cast in the same popular style.

One of Luther's most cherished desires was to see all of the common folk involved in the singing of the new spiritual folksongs. Hugo Leichtentritt calls Luther "the originator of the ideas, [who] knew how to inspire artists of rank to write in a style adapted to the character of the Protestant Creed."[7]

Once begun, Lutheran hymns multiplied and were eagerly caught up by the people. Luther gathered fine musicians around him and asked for their help in writing hymns after some of his earlier models. Often hymns and tunes were printed on single sheets and carried all over Germany by wandering students and peddlers. Ninde writes:

> The new evangel, like a voice from the skies, coupled with the strong human touch of the hymns, appealed to both heart and soul. They [the hymns] were used not only in church, but, an eyewitness wrote, "The artisan sings them at his work, the maid as she washes the clothes, the peasant on his furrow, the mother to the child that cries in the cradle." Cases are on record where whole towns were so moved that the people in a

---

6. Hugo Leichtentritt, *Music, History and Ideas,* p. 105.
7. Ibid.

body went over to the new faith. No wonder that indignant Romanites declared that "Luther's songs have damned more souls than all his books and speeches."[8]

The tunes which the Lutherans used were largely responsible for the popularity of the songs. There was as much spontaneity in the melodies as in the texts. These tunes were selected from various sources, such as old Latin hymns and secular melodies in use among the Bohemian Brethren. In some cases, changes were made, as necessary, to adapt old tunes to new texts.

Lutheran hymns enjoyed widespread popularity because they filled a vacuum in people's lives. For centuries the people had to be content to listen to the clergy do the singing; when the people did sing, more often than not, the popular religious songs were addressed to the Virgin Mary, the Eucharist, or the saints, not to God or to other people as songs of Christian experience. As Luther personalized the hymns, he also popularized them for the people of his day.

There are distinct differences between the Reformation movement of the sixteenth century and the evangelistic movements of today. Indeed, the Protestant Reformation was not strictly evangelistic, as we define evangelism, since the Reformation in Germany was complicated by political and social issues. There was, however, a basic spiritual import to the movement.

Today's church musician can learn a great deal from Luther's musical approach and practice. Luther used a great variety of musical styles to good advantage in order to attract, communicate with, and hold his followers. His music was music to which the people could readily relate. But can Luther's situation be compared to the situation in today's churches as the minister of music attempts to attract, witness, and communicate? If Luther were on the scene today, says Harold Best,

he would have to reckon with new factors. He would have to examine the practice of borrowing in the light of a distance

---

8. Ninde, *Nineteen Centuries of Christian Song,* p. 62.

between the Church and secular culture unlike anything he had to face. He would have to confront an unprecedented proliferation of musical styles from both within and without Western culture, and he would have to face the Church with its preference for provincial witness. He would undoubtedly recognize that a large part of our musical experience is depersonalized, issuing electronically from walls, ceilings and earphones as a background for everything from shopping to worshipping.[9]

We are aware of the enthusiasm of the Protestant Reformation and realize the importance of the chorales as a reflection of that enthusiasm. But in spite of the magnificent sound of these chorales when performed today, we cannot think of this music as an accurate reflection of the Reformation, for the style of the chorale tune has evolved dramatically since the sixteenth century. Tunes which were once very natural, syncopated, and singable, were arranged to such a degree, especially by nineteenth century "meddlers," that much of the spark, spontaneity, and vitality were removed. In the period of the Reformation, this music was directly associated with popular idioms, carols, and Meistersinger music.

Erik Routley well observes that probably no person in church music history has gone as far as Luther did in crossing the "forbidden frontier between sacred and secular music." The Lutheran philosophy, as paraphrased by Routley, was, "Let it be music; we will make it as sacred as it need be."[10]

John Calvin

In contrast to Luther, John Calvin (1509–1564) was not an artist, but a stern disciplinarian, and the most systematic of the Reformers. His view of music in the church can be summarized by the following basic points:

1. Music is for the people, so it must be simple.
2. Music is for God, so it must be modest.
3. Simplicity and modesty are best attained by music of the unaccompanied voice.

---

9. Harold Best, "The Climate of Creativity," p. 4.

10. Routley, *Music Leadership in the Church,* p. 89.

Thus we can begin to discern a developing doctrine of "sacred music." Calvin was antiprofessional in his view toward the ministry of music. There were to be no choirs or musical instruments; there could be only that music in which everyone could participate—*in unison*—using strictly the Psalms. In Geneva, Calvin used vernacular "Psalms in meter," utilizing tunes that were sarcastically called "Geneva Jiggs." Many of these tunes were derived from German and French folk music. Even the earliest melodies associated with the Genevan Psalter were, in many cases, familiar ballad tunes. By 1540, Psalms were being sung by children and adults, in the French palace and in the fields, by the royal family and their servants, and they were sung to familiar secular airs.

Fortunately, Calvin's path crossed with those of Louis Bourgeois, a fine musical artist, and Clement Marot, a court poet. Marot (and later Théodore de Bèze) produced some beautiful lyric poetry, and Bourgeois used secular sources for some of his tunes (though not the same sources that the Lutherans used).

The exclusive use of psalmody appears stern and severe to the contemporary churchman, but Calvinism produced what was probably one of the most popular forms of corporate praise in history. Furthermore, in the process, Calvin kept the doctrine pure through the strict use of Scripture while popularizing it by using common and desirable tunes. In the metrical Psalms, the people had fresh versions of the Scripture turned into well-known ballad meters and set to music. In this way, Scripture was easily learned because it was framed in a familiar pattern. Here at last were sacred songs which belonged not only to the clergy and to the "religious" in the monasteries, but which were the possession of all the people.

Reformation Music in England

Next to the English Bible and the Book of Common Prayer, the metrical Psalms were probably the most influential literary contribution made by the Reformation to the religious life of the English people. As Henry Foote indicates, "they were accepted with enthusiasm and spread like wildfire."[11] There is also no doubt that the metrical text exerted a far greater influence among the common people than did the prose text. The influence was intensified by the association of the verses with the melodies that accompanied them.

In England, the psalters and Psalm-singing were very popular. But, as Ninde writes, the roots of popular sacred English song can be traced back as far as Anglo-Saxon days,

> when the gleesome, wandering minstrels sang knightly tales and sacred story; when, twelve centuries ago, Aldhelm, devout and gifted bishop, stood at a bridgehead and sang his own songs, and then preached to the crowd of listeners. We think of John Wyclif and his followers. They were nicknamed "lollards," perhaps from a word meaning "to sing softly" and suggesting that they sang as well as preached in the tongue of the common people.[12]

The first echoes of the new movement to cross the English Channel from the Continent were from Lutheran Germany. However, England was hardly prepared for many of the drastic musical changes that Germany quite readily accepted. Thus it was Calvin rather than Luther who set the musical model on British soil. The Psalm, instead of the hymn, came into use both in England and Scotland (and afterward in America), and it continued to be favored for over two hundred years.

During the reign of Queen Elizabeth, the singing of "Geneva Jiggs" became almost a passion, with the Psalms sung not just in church but in the street. Bailey has said of this tradition,

> Singing thus became a powerful instrument of propaganda for the reformed faith, whether Established Puritan or Dissenting. In Cromwell's day (1649–58), when the Puritans were in power, the Psalms were set to popular tunes and jiggs which were "too good for the devil," and were sung everywhere—at

---

11. Henry W. Foote, "Recent American Hymnody," p. 23.

12. Ninde, *Nineteen Centuries of Christian Song,* p. 81.

Lord Mayor's dinners, by soldiers on the march and at parade, and by families who had windows fronting on the streets.[13]

The writers of most of the Psalm tunes remained anonymous. These composers drew from the repertoire of popular tunes, finding nothing wrong with using a phrase which had been used before. Many of the Psalm tunes contained clichés, but the best of them had a quality that placed them above the commonplace. We can be reasonably sure that the tunes were improvised by the people from the musical vocabulary of the time, and it was no great issue to the early Psalm-singers that stock phrases occurred again and again.

The influence of the Psalter is incalculable. The exalted language of the Psalms became the familiar pattern of much Christian thought and speech, and the people's taste in music took firm control. The tunes were simple, popular, and sung in unison. Yet they were definitely church music, as can be seen when comparing them with contemporary carols or secular tunes. The Psalm tunes were more sedate, more serene, less driving, and less dancelike than the typical secular tunes.

The Lutherans came closer to purely secular styles than did the English church musicians. The British were able to create a melodic style which was distinct from both traditional church and secular styles, but which still managed to be a "folk style." In fact, the Psalm tunes became almost national anthems in Scotland. In style, some of the tunes (particularly in the Scottish Psalter) were derived from late medieval processionals, originating from sources such as the *Laudi spirituali,* somewhat between the sacred and the secular.

Effects of Lutheran and Calvinist Music

In comparing the effects of Lutheran and Calvinistic positions on music, we must note that Luther was liberal and permissive, while Calvin was restrictive, controlling, and regulating—acting as an opponent of professional church music.

---

13. Bailey, *The Gospel in Hymns,* p. 13.

In a discussion comparing these two Reformers, Routley states:

> Vicious caricature from the Roman church is quite unable to represent him [Luther], as it represents Calvin, as dry, heartless, and stonily puritanical, because his manner of life and thought was in truth the reverse of puritanical. Luther's theology was not a theology of negation; by definition it was the opposite of a theology of legalism.[14]

The music of both major Reformation systems was well-received, however. In Geneva the acceptance came because of the direction of "professionals" such as Louis Bourgeois. In Lutheran territory the overwhelming majority of the music succeeded because of its reliance on the (cruder) virtues of the folk song.

Erik Routley claims to detect a paradox regarding the comparative results of both musical "systems."[15] He asserts that if more of Luther's music had survived, we would be inclined to say that Luther was "right." Routley maintains that Lutheran chorales had great success even into the eighteenth century, and that the Genevan Psalm had a much shorter life—he admits, however, that this alone cannot serve as "proof" of who had the better music. But Routley fails to acknowledge that the Geneva Psalter yielded various English and Scottish Psalters and that the Psalter remained the principal songbook for English and American congregations into the nineteenth century. In fact, the Psalter is still the main source of corporate singing in a number of denominations (e.g., the Scottish Presbyterians).

Historical data suggest that Calvin's restrictiveness produced a smaller quantity of performance music, which, although of high quality, was limited to a more local use. Musical development was not encouraged, so less was created. It seems that Luther's permissiveness, on the other hand, helped his music of the people to increase and become widely used. Calvin's insistence that the only professionals

14. Routley, *The Church and Music*, p. 118.
15. Ibid., pp. 118–19.

allowed in church leadership be clergy and elders tended to stifle any enduring popular and professional music.

The Counter-Reformation

Humanism in the last half of the sixteenth century began to separate the individual from the church. A disparity developed between sacred and secular life, and between certain intellectual viewpoints. Sacred music was increasingly influenced by the rise of Protestantism and the opposing measures of the Counter-Reformation. New Protestant attitudes created a new body of music for Protestant use, and the Catholic repertoire—particularly in Italy and Spain—also responded to changes in musical taste. Josquin Deprès and Orlando di Lasso had made wide use of the French, Dutch, and Italian secular song as the basis for sacred music.

A generation before the Council of Trent, Erasmus said,

> We have introduced an artificial and theatrical music into the church, a bawling and agitation of various voices, such as I believe had never been heard in the theatres of the Greeks and Romans. Horns, trumpets, pipes vie and sound along constantly with the voices. Amorous and lascivious melodies are heard such as elsewhere accompany only the dances of courtesans and clowns. The people run into the churches as if they were theatres, for the sake of the sensuous charm of the ear.[16]

The Council of Trent (1545–63) convened to deal primarily with liturgical abuses and only secondarily with music. Final statements by the Council were generally negative, making few specific recommendations for the improvement of the church's music. The Council merely forbade particular practices and insisted that certain results be obtained, without specifying the means.[17]

In September, 1562, a committee drew up a resolution which dealt with music for use in the Mass.

---

16. Cited in Reese, *Music in the Renaissance*, p. 448.
17. Ibid., p. 449.

All things should indeed be so ordered that the Masses
... may reach tranquilly into the ears and hearts of those
who hear them, when everything is executed clearly and at
the right speed.... Let nothing profane be intermingled, but
only hymns and divine praises. The whole plan of singing
... should not ... give empty pleasure to the ear, but in
such a way that the words may be clearly understood by
all.... They shall also banish from church all music that contains, whether in the singing or in the organ playing, things
that are lascivious or impure.[18]

The reference to the importance of the words being understood was an obvious criticism of the polyphony common at
the time. But after the appointing of several committees and
many hours of deliberation, there was a partial victory for
polyphonic music. It was to be permitted, but in accordance
with church and humanistic ideals.

Though the Council of Trent forbade the use of secular
melodies as *cantus firmi* in Masses, composers, in order to
avoid detection of secular material, wrote Masses which were
sine nomine or *sine titulo*. But in Germany, parody Masses
continued to adapt music of the liveliest kind. In many cases,
the titles of the models are unhesitatingly given in the titles
of the Masses.[19]

While the Reformers were busy influencing the population
with the teaching and evangelizing ministry of their music,
the Roman Catholic church was not sitting idly by. Catholic
composers changed and flaunted the techniques of their
music. Because they felt they had a proud history of quality
art music in their churches, they chose not to follow the
practice of Luther in using the popular idioms of the day. The
Roman church began an impressive display of their great and
learned art and music. They placed great emphasis on the
spectacular, using their heritage of great artistic music in impressive concerts, parades, and productions.

At St. Mark's in Venice, Andrea and Giovanni Gabrieli
used colorful antiphonal music for both choirs and instrumental ensembles, and at St. Peter's, Girolamo Frescobaldi

---

18. Ibid.
19. Ibid., p. 451.

was drawing throngs of people to hear his organ-playing. Music occupied

> a unique place in Elizabethan society, both in the church and in the home. Jesuit priests from the *Collegium germanicum* in Rome were bringing the Passion Music of the Spanish monk Victoria into Germany, to be passed on to Heinrich Schutz, Hassler, Bach and others. Jesuits were also making use of opera and ballet as counter-attractions in connection with the Counter-Reformation.[20]

In his theosophical book, *The Influence of Music on History and Morals, a Vindication of Plato,* Cyril Scott claims that in the years following the flowering of the Reformation, the Neapolitan melodies of Scarlatti "made religion more attractive" and thus "coordinated church and the home."[21] Therefore, the attempt of the Roman church was to make the church—and religion—more attractive to the people through the use of more sophisticated, "professional" music.

The rise of the "professional" church musician always meant an increase in the secularization of the church music style. This does not refer, in the instance of the Counter-Reformation, to a marketplace secularization, but rather to an artistic secularization. Good examples are found in the music of the Gabrielis and Frescobaldi. Another example is the eighteenth-century Anglican church's heavy use of Purcell and even Handel. The same kind of music was written for sacred and secular occasions. As a result of this influence, church music became much more metrical and dancelike; the beat was regular, reminiscent of a march or a minuet.

The part played by hymns in the Roman Catholic tradition was far different from the part played in most Protestant systems. Generally, the hymns of the Roman Catholics were used at Benediction and popular evangelistic services. The Protestant groups that stood furthest from the Roman Catholic tradition (Reformed churches, the Independents, Presbyterians, and Baptists) instead used hymns as an integral part of their public worship.

---

20. Allen, *Philosophies of Music History,* p. 28.
21. Cited in ibid., p. 61.

Following the Reformation the Roman Catholic hymns also imitated the prevailing idiom of the time. Rarely, however, do we find the hymns of the Roman Catholics taking any stand against poor musical standards the way we find in Protestant hymnody.[22] Catholic hymnody may have leaned toward the popular folk song style following the Reformation, but the Catholic hymn never really established a church style. The *Mirfield Mission Hymn Book* is filled with popular tunes which affected Catholic hymn tune styles for some time. According to Routley:

> It is the Catholic counterpart to English revivalistic music; and its popularity is due to the same cause, that both English revival music and Catholic hymnody are only very loosely connected with any kind of ceremonial liturgy.[23]

Thus, the strength and influence of the Reformers also brought about an indirect change in the music of the Catholic church. There was, however, an important difference between the two musical systems. The Reformers brought folk music which could be sung by the people in the church services. In the Catholic church there was more "artistic" and "professional" influence in the music, but the common people still did not have a chance to participate in worship. The Reformation music became more "spiritualized," though it was sung by the people, while the Roman Catholic changes brought about more secularization. The music was written and performed by the "professional" musician, to whom music was merely an art form.

The Seventeenth Century: Sethus Calvisius

The seventeenth century saw great changes in most musical idioms, and several new musicians and musical philosophers received recognition. One of these was Sethus Calvisius, an admirer of Luther and his work. Like Luther, Calvisius wanted to simplify and popularize the music of the

---

22. Erik Routley, *The Music of Christian Hymnody,* p. 151.
23. Ibid., p. 155.

church.[24] Calvisius was interested not only in the ancient beginnings of music, but in its meaning for him as a practical musician, composer, and teacher. He believed in the musical art of his day, and he wanted to show the value of its precepts and conventions. He was unusual for his time in that he admired much in the music of his contemporaries—including Luther—and his immediate predecessors. In fact, says Blume:

> The attributing of anonymous songs to Luther (which also reflected a veneration of him that was becoming almost mythical) finally reached its climax in Seth Calvisius, whose song book presented no fewer than 137 texts and melodies as genuine works of Luther.[25]

Theorists interested in the origins of music had not connected their theories with contemporary practice, except to condemn it. And conversely, composers with new ideas (and their defenders) were not apt to bother with ancient theory. Calvisius wanted to be progressive while acknowledging the historical, theoretical background of music. He accepted the theory of music's divine origin in the first utterance of man at creation, but he also saw progress, as men inherited accumulated musical tradition and passed on worthy contributions of their own. Thus, Calvisius found a balance between the philosophy of music and the practicality of music for the people. Calvisius found very little room in his music for fancy, hearsay, and supersitition, factors coming strongly into play in the seventeenth century. It would profit many church musicians today to consider the balance between musical heritage and popular idioms which was characteristic of Calvisius.

Mysticism and Pietism

After the Thirty Years' War (1618–48), many Lutherans turned to mysticism and Pietism. These surging movements of popular devotion to Christ, involving the worship of the mysteries of God, were exemplified in the hymns of Paul

24. Allen, *Philosophies of Music History,* pp. 5–10.
25. Blume, *Protestant Church Music,* p. 45.

Gerhardt, sometimes called "the Charles Wesley of Germany." Pietism emphasized the importance of personal devotion and plain, serious reverence. The movement was led by Philip Spener (1635–1705), an ordained Lutheran pastor. Pietism avoided high churchmanship and concentrated upon good will. The music of public praise in Germany was strongly influenced by Pietism. Inasmuch as Pietism was essentially private, so Pietistic music was essentially private music. It was largely sacred art music of the cultivated musician, much like that of the salon and opera house.

The seventeenth century brought about changes in the performance practices of the psalters and chorales of the Reformation. Soon after new secular-type tunes were introduced to the psalters of the later seventeenth century, most of them were "deliberately lengthened out by giving their notes equal length, and singing was slowed down in the supposed interest of solemnity."[26] This same treatment was given the tunes and settings used by the Germans. During the seventeenth century the music and words of hymns and Psalms became more "spiritualized" than secularized because of the strong religious philosophies which emphasized "religiosity" and "solemnity."

Oratorio

From the seventeenth and eighteenth centuries came the oratorio. Though it was not necessarily used for outreach, it provides another example of biblical stories being transformed into live and lively, secular-style entertainment. The first oratorios were composed and performed in Italy, and were sung in Latin. The earliest examples provided a legal alternative to opera attendance during the Lenten season.

Many oratorios, such as those of Giacomo Carissimi (1605–1674), were aristocratic in nature, and exhibited a more devotional style. Later, however, as the oratorio became more vernacular and spread to other countries, some of the most popular devices of the time—those of opera—were employed. Except for the fact that oratorios were generally .

---

26. Foote, "Recent American Hymnody," p. 15.

performed without staging and were concerned with Bible stories, they were practically indistinguishable from opera. Alan Rich asserts that "they are, but for the solemnity of their subject matter and their lack of staging, genuine musical dramas."[27] Thus, the oratorio shows the cyclic return of the secularized Bible story in the form of drama, in much the same way drama had appeared in the Middle Ages.

Conclusion

Only a few selected facets of sixteenth- and seventeenth-century church music have been studied in this chapter. In considering the outreach music of the Reformers, we can see that they used the secular, popular tunes of the day as settings for spreading their doctrine. Conversely, the Counter-Reformation made its music more effective and attractive by building on an already-strong tradition. The Reformers secularized their music by using the familiar tunes of the common man, while the Counter-Reformers secularized their music by using professional composers who wrote in the idiom of the classical art forms.

In the seventeenth century, the pendulum swung more toward the use of sacred music by those who believed in the spiritualization of Biblical subjects. Yet much of the music remained that of the layman, since the mystics and Pietists used their music almost exclusively in personal devotion and expression. By the end of the seventeenth century, the oratorio came into respected prominence and greatly resembled the earlier form of the liturgical dramas and mysteries of the Middle Ages.

---

27. Rich, "Religion with a Rock Beat," p. 19.

Chapter 4

Eighteenth-Century Church Music

During the eighteenth century, music again functioned as an important tool in mass evangelism. Thousands were led to Christian decision and commitment through the songs of several revival movements, most notably, the Wesleyan and Welsh.

Much of the church music of the century was distant and ceremonial, not penetrating the depths of human experience and feeling. The better composers wrote church music either incidentally or not at all. Many composers of far less talent tried to express subjective religious ideas by using some of the more superficial qualities of classical music. This resulted in a music which became increasingly emotional and individualistic, and in a church music which became, by the Victorian era, an artistic disaster.

As the eighteenth century continued, the stage was being set musically, psychologically, and emotionally for one of the most personal, subjective, and emotional trends in the history of church music.

Isaac Watts

One of the great eighteenth-century leaders in church hymnody was Isaac Watts (1674–1748). Watts believed firmly in the duty of singing in the worship of God. He also felt that singing should represent God's Word to man. He blamed the prevalent lack of interest in church singing on the exclusive use of Psalms. He stated:

> I have long been convinced, that one great Occasion of this evil arises from the Matter and Words to which we confine all our songs. Some of 'em are almost opposite to the Spirit of the Gospel: Many of them foreign to the State of the New Testament, and widely different from the present circumstances of Christians. . . . When we are just entering into an Evangelical Frame by some of the Glories of the Gospel presented in the brightest figures of Judaism, yet the very next line perhaps which the Clerk parcels out unto us, hath something in it so extremely Jewish and cloudy, that darkens our sight of God the Saviour.[1]

In large part, Watts's hymns are rhymed theology—a theology derived from John Calvin. In subsequent years, as certain Christian movements have diverged from Calvinism, many of the hymns of Watts have been altered. A. E. Bailey has summarized the fundamental theological views of Watts as seen in his hymns:

1. God is an absolute and arbitrary ruler.
2. Man is totally depraved.
3. All children are supposed to fall under considerable conviction of sin.
4. The only relief from despair lies in the thought that Jesus has paid the penalty of sin, and that if I am among the fortunate "elect" I shall be rescued by Him.[2]

Watts's poetry was easily understood by the average person of his day. Though Watts could be very learned and intricate in his writings (as was evident in some of his earlier published poems), he realized that if hymns were to serve the common person they had to be simple. His meters were the standard common, long, and short. His utter simplicity is one of the reasons his hymns almost completely dominated Dissenting church hymnody for 150 years.

---

1. Cited in Edwin H. Hughes, *Worship in Music,* p. 73.
2. Bailey, *The Gospel in Hymns,* pp. 57–58.

Also, his hymns appealed to the senses. Images were produced which were familiar to ordinary people. The hymns were often emotional and compassionate, and even his Calvinistic doctrine took on a certain warmth. Bailey said of his hymns, "Christ is full of human sympathy that evokes from the individual a personal response; man is filled with hope or fear, with joy or penitence."[3]

Because of his Calvinistic theology, Watts seldom extended an invitation for salvation in his hymn texts, although such a theme was not unknown in his writings. There is one hymn under the heading of "The Invitation of the Gospel" which begins:

> Let every mortal ear attend
> And every heart rejoice;
> The trumpet of the Gospel sounds
> With an inviting voice.

The first verse of one of his hymns under the heading "Christ's Invitation to Sinners" says,

> Come hither all ye weary souls,
> Ye heavy laden sinners, come,
> I'll give you rest from all your toils
> And raise you to my heavenly home.

Isaac Watts was not unfriendly to the revival movement of the Wesleys, but he was too early to be caught up in it. For many years after Methodism began, the Wesley hymns were written only for Wesleyan followers and were sung almost exclusively by Wesleyans. This gave their hymns a sectarian tone, and for a time it hindered their use by the general Protestant public. Other hymnists of the eighteenth century were divided between the two traditions. Some followed Watts, while others became part of the new evangelism, having taken up the musical movement begun by Charles Wesley.

---

3. Ibid., p. 61.

Moravian Pietism as Background for the Wesleys

Passing mention should be made of the tireless work of Count Nicholas Ludwig von Zinzendorf (1700–1760), who brought revival to Pietism by instilling some of the earlier zeal of John Hus. Zinzendorf's evangelical fervor brought revival, not to Pietistic churches, but to individuals. The tremendous number of "spiritual songs" he wrote were not designed for congregational singing, but for family and individual use.

Historically, this tradition had great influence on the Wesleyan revival. Not only did Zinzendorf write hymns, but he had an important effect on the music of John and Charles Wesley. These evangelical revivalists learned from Zinzendorf the power of sacred song. At an early age, John Wesley organized among his schoolboy companions the "Order of the Mustard Seed," planning to do Christian service, especially in heathen countries. Later Zinzendorf carried his missionary ventures far and wide, even spending three years in Pennsylvania.

The Music of the Wesleyan Revivals

The Wesleyan revival was the first of several eighteenth-century revivals, and it was much more than a local, emotional, and transient movement. John Wesley, like most revivalists, "was a fighter, but he did not, like most others, rely primarily for his message on the denunciation of abuses. He relied on an ancient Gospel of power, wrath and mercy."[4]

John Wesley had his contact with Zinzendorf and the Moravians while he was still in his thirties, and it was from these people that he learned the potential of evangelization through music. Wesleyan evangelism, however, was different from that of Zinzendorf. Though Wesleyan hymns were, as Zinzendorf's, totally individual, they were also entirely theological. One need only survey Charles Wesley's nearly seven thousand hymns for evidence of this. But Charles Wesley was probably more skilled as a theologian than a musician. His genius was in knowing just enough of the principles of

---

4. Routley, *The Church and Music*, p. 159.

music to recognize what kind of music was best for his purposes.

The several musical editions of the Wesleyan hymnbooks of the eighteenth century show a large number of very singable, triple-time melodies which are replete with ornaments and appoggiaturas, suggesting an instrumental idiom. Some of these melodies were derived from secular sources, but most of them were composed especially for the hymn texts by anonymous musicians. The Wesleys insisted that the music be amicable to the people. The frequent use of sequences and tunes with few melodic skips made the music of and for the people. Most of the hymns were easily sung and learned at their first hearing. This was democratic church music—even more democratic than that of either Calvin or Luther, since the theology of the Wesleys acknowledged a wider potential for redemption, enabling them to make broad use of secular idioms.

Evangelistic hymns in the modern sense were by-products of Britain's "Great Awakening." The preaching of John and Charles Wesley and the underlying tenets of the Dutch theologian Jacob Arminius (1560–1609) eventually led to the creation of the first "invitation" songs. Calvinism rarely generated songs of invitation. These would appear later, particularly during the Finney meetings of the nineteenth century.

The Wesleys, however, approached evangelism with the new view of a "sovereignty of man" with regard to his personal salvation. In Arminian theology an individual has the power to accept or reject God's offer of salvation. One of Charles Wesley's hymns says:

> Come, sinners, to the Gospel feast;
> Let every soul be Jesus' guest;
> Ye need not one be left behind,
> For God hath bidden all mankind.
> This is the time; no more delay!
> This is the Lord's accepted day;
> Come thou, this moment, at His call,
> And live for Him Who died for all.

Musically, Wesleyan hymnody is responsible for expanding hymns from the two-line meters—common, long, and short. For the musical sources they used Psalm tunes, opera songs, and folk songs. According to Donald Hustad, the Wesley texts "were fundamental for early Methodist theology. They also covered every conceivable aspect of Christian devotional experience and may be said to be the progenitors of the modern gospel songs."[5]

The Wesleys greatly enriched the stores of English hymns, by modifying existing hymns and establishing new hymns in which a note of evangelism was heard. These new hymns of Christian experience opened the way for many similar expressions. Such hymns of personal testimony have been a popular form of sacred music ever since the time of the Wesleys.

John Wesley was interested in bringing hymn singing to America. Gilbert Chase notes that Wesley's "chief concern in the colonies was to spread the Gospel, and also to introduce the rather radical practice of hymn singing to which he had been converted by his contact with the Moravians."[6] Though the hymns of Watts were gaining favor, psalmody was still the dominant music in colonial church practice. However, John Wesley's 1737 publication, *A Collection of Psalms and Hymns,* was a translation of German hymns.

Wesley continued to attend the meetings of the Moravians after his return to London in 1738. This led to his reading of Luther's *Preface to the Epistle to the Romans,* during which time he was converted. An entrance in his journal relates that he felt his heart "strangely warmed. I felt I did trust in Christ, Christ alone for salvation, and an assurance was given me that He had taken away my sins, even mine, and saved me from the law of sin and death."[7] This was, as it turned out, the basic gospel text for nearly all of Wesley's evangelical revivalistic hymnody. These kinds of emotional reactions, along with this response toward conversion and salvation, and the imagery of sin and condemnation, are the roots from which came American folk hymns.

---

5. Donald Hustad, "Music and the Church's Outreach," pp. 177–86.
6. Gilbert Chase, *America's Music: From the Pilgrims to the Present,* p. 45.
7. Ibid. Quoting from the journal of John Wesley.

According to Arthur Stevenson:

> The reason why Methodism was so successful in the beginning of its history was that it presented the view of the Gospel for which it stood in the language of the people when it addressed them in language wedded to music that the people sang without special training. It does not seem to have changed nor sought to have changed the standard of musical taste of its day. . . .
>
> It does not appear, however, that the old-time tunes of early Methodism were the choral tunes to which most of the standard lyrics are now set, but folk-tunes that the people knew, or such as were built on the same pattern of musical construction.[8]

Wesley's England was ready for revival. The nation—and other revivalists—was standing ready for someone to take a position of leadership. Routley supports this view:

> All great historical figures are sons as well as fathers; they grow out of history as well as influencing it. . . . Men were ready for direction. George Whitefield, Martin Madan, John Cennick, Selina, Countess of Huntingdon and, of course, his own brother Charles were waiting for the word from John Wesley.
>
> Apart from divine providence and human helpers, the strongest agent for the propagation of Wesley's message was music. . . .
>
> A message that is to be forced home to individual men can be immensely strengthened by simple, melodic music; this is especially true of a message which proclaims certainty and safety rather than the answers to sophisticated intellectual problems.[9]

The Wesleys had several musical traditions from which to choose. One was the Psalm tradition; but by this time it was a dying form. The practices of Restoration music were also available; but the other, more important idiom for their use was the new Italian opera style, particularly that of Handel. The historical timing was very near perfect. Just as a vigor-

---

8. Arthur L. Stevenson, *The Story of Southern Hymnology,* p. 46.
9. Routley, *The Music of Christian Hymnody,* p. 91.

ous, new, entertaining medium was being sought, one became readily available.

John Wesley was not always pleased with the development of the music of his followers. In his preface to *Select Hymns for Christians of All Denominations,* he counseled his readers to

> Learn *those* tunes before any others;
> Sing them exactly as they are printed;
> Sing lustily; sing all of them;
> Sing modestly; sing in tune;
> Above all, sing spiritually.

Regarding some of this undesirable music which had crept into the Wesleyan music, Routley has said, "We must accept the fact that the generous and hospitable Gospel of the Wesleys allowed a good deal of bogus music to slip in."[10]

Methodist music, as a music of the people and for the people, tended to shy away from serious art music. The lyric, florid tunes are supported by little harmonic and contrapuntal interest. Harmony and counterpoint take the line of least resistance. There is a predominance of the sweet sounds of parallel thirds and sixths, and a noticeable absence of musical tension and challenge. Many of the Wesleyan tunes run high in spirit; it is sometimes difficult, however, to distinguish between the high spirits and hysteria, and between the warmth of the gospel and the fever of enthusiasm. This style was influential throughout England with nearly all the dissenting movements utilizing the new music.

Although the nineteenth century was to be the heyday of church music amateurism in most of England and Europe, the root causes for this are found in the eighteenth century. In 1793, Richard Eastcott had this to say of the Wesleyan music:

> It has been said, and I believe with great truth, that many of the converts among the Methodists have declared that the singing was their primary attraction. If we are sensible of the great efficacy of this system of the Methodists in gaining proselytes, surely there can be no reason why the established

---

10. Ibid., p. 96.

church and other places of worship should not adopt it. Every warrantable method it is undoubtedly ours most strenuously to pursue; by first warming the affections, we shall afterwards have an opportunity of convincing the understanding; and if we are happy enough to make a convert, it matters but little, whether the primary attraction was sound or sense, provided we retain him by producing irrefragable arguments in favor of the faith he hath embraced.[11]

The tunes used with many of the Wesley texts were frequently popular ones, less inhibited melodically and rhythmically than the straightforward Psalm tunes, and these new songs were sung with great enthusiasm and vitality. This practice provided the foundation for evangelical folk hymns which became so important in both evangelism and worship in the English-speaking world. The tunes were familiar folk melodies which everyone could sing, with words that spoke the language of the layman.

Speaking of Charles Wesley's songs, Myra and Merrill state:

he tried them out, of course, at the end of his brother John's sermons, when he was expected to have a new song ready. Like Watts, he didn't write tunes (he didn't have time); "it was Wesley's practice to seize upon any song of the theater or the street, the moment it became popular, and make it carry some newly written hymn into the homes of the people," says hymnographer Silas H. Paine. He picked up some of Handel's classical melodies and got criticized for being too "worldly."[12]

The Causes and Significance
of the Wesleyan Movement

It has been established that evangelical music has always been tied to a corresponding awakening of evangelical fervor. After the praise hymns of Isaac Watts and his contemporaries, the Wesleys appeared with their hymns of personal religious experience. Parallel to the Wesleys' rise, and to a large degree the force behind the social changes, was the

---

11. Cited in Wienandt, *Opinions on Church Music,* p. 101.
12. Harold Hyra and Dean Merrill, *Rock, Bach, and Superschlock,* p. 93.

"Great Awakening" with its concern for the individual. The Methodist hymns, and the gospel inherent in them, were a reflection of the social and religious backgrounds of the great upheaval.

In 1660, the Anglican Church in England was reinstated to full power following the period of Oliver Cromwell and the Commonwealth. The church was a staunch supporter of the monarch from whom it received its privileges and power. Ambitious men, whatever their abilities, sought and bought the high positions in the church. These well-placed men were becoming wealthier while the average citizen was becoming poorer. For a time, dissenting clergymen provided a protesting voice in the established church, but in 1662 the Dissenters were cast out. After that, the only workers for morality and religion were on the outside looking in and the efforts of reform were largely stopped. But even the Dissenters, with the token amount of toleration they were beginning to enjoy, were less aggressive on some of these issues than they once had been. With much of the persecution over, they had no strong objection to the present state of affairs. Albert Bailey points out that

> Watts was enjoying a comfortable living in the home of a rich merchant and fighting for a renovated Psalmody and a Gospel hymnody for Church people, the "elect" of the Calvinistic creed. He had no idea that the business of the Church was to seek and save the lost and remake the social structure of the world.[13]

In the fifty years before the flourishing of the Wesleys and Whitefield, England had reached a low point in morality. When the three evangelists accepted the challenge of this dark situation, they were instrumental in achieving social reform. They did not approach the problem from an economic or social viewpoint, but from that of the gospel. According to Bailey:

> They believed that the Spirit of God could change the hearts of men, could make them desire a better life here, and

13. Bailey, *The Gospel in Hymns,* p. 74.

trusting in the saving power of God through Christ, could break the chains of sin and cause them to rise to a sobriety and dignity which was theirs by right. Historians can trace the revolutionary effects of their preaching in all fields: personal morality, health, politics, the penal code, class barriers, economic and personal slavery, education, literature, music and the religious life of all sects.[14]

Charles Wesley's conversion resulted in an immediate outburst of song. He composed verses nearly every day, no matter where he was. He wrote almost seven thousand hymns, on hundreds of Scripture verses, dealing with nearly every aspect of Christian experience and Methodist theology.

John Wesley's primary contribution to hymnody was as editor, organizer, and publisher of his brother's hymns. John selected and published hymn-tracts in both large and small collections, grouping them according to subject. In fifty-three years he published a total of fifty-six such collections. The smaller, less expensive collections were used in revival services. Under the direction of John Wesley, Methodist hymnody became the most powerful tool of evangelism England ever knew.

The Wesleys were fully aware that reformation had to come to English society. In France it took the force of a bloody revolution to free the lower classes and assure social reform. Historians recognize that the Wesleys were an important influence in thwarting a bloody revolution in England. John and Charles Wesley spoke forcibly against the multitude of evils of their day, and their music played a very important part in this reforming work.

In any period of revival there are antagonists toward the musical idioms, and the Wesleyan revival was no exception. Most of the religious people of the eighteenth century, whether part of the established church or not, were Calvinists, including Isaac Watts, whose hymns were tremendously popular. This made the Arminian Wesleys quite unpopular in many circles. Bailey explains:

> While, therefore, Watts can praise God and Christ for the salvation which he (fortunately) was elected to receive, he has

---

14. Ibid., p. 76.

no word of invitation to sinners, just as in his preaching he
had no passion for the saving of souls. But the Wesleys were
on fire for saving souls, and their hymns pleaded with sinners
to come to the Water of Life.[15]

There are even evidences of Charles Wesley taking a swipe at
Calvinism, as in this hymn:

> Ah, gentle, gracious Dove,
> And art thou grieved in me?
> That sinners should restrain thy love
> And say, "It is not free;
> It is not free for all;
> The most thou passest by,
> And mockest with a fruitless call
> Whom thou hast doomed to die."
> O Horrible Decree,
> Worthy of whence it came!
> Forgive their hellish blasphemy
> Who charge it on the Lamb,
> Whose pity him inclined
> To leave His throne above,
> The Friend and Saviour of mankind,
> The God of grace and love.[16]

Other Eighteenth-Century
Evangelical Leaders

John Newton (1725–1807)

John Newton was an evangelical with a great personal devotion to Christ and an earnest desire to see men saved.
Salvaged from an infamous background of slave-trading, he
attracted many people with his sincere interest in them, his
earnest preaching, and his reputation as a shady-character-
turned-good.

Musically, he caused controversy because he used hymns
instead of the Sternhold and Hopkins psalter. This was a
most unusual practice for an Anglican. But Newton did not
find the simplicity and warmth he wanted to express even in

---

15. Ibid., p. 89.
16. "God's Everlasting Love" (1741), quoted in ibid., p. 90.

Watts, and therefore began to write his own hymns. To this task he brought his friend and neighbor, William Cowper, and their book *The Olney Hymns* was published in 1779. This was a collection of revival hymns to be used for didactic instruction in the evangelical faith. (For Newton and Cowper, religious education was of greater importance than the conversion of sinners.)

The Countess of Huntingdon (1707–91)

Selina, Countess of Huntingdon, was a gifted woman who for fifty years was a benefactress of evangelical preachers and hymn-writers, both Dissenting and Anglican. She knew and supported the Wesleys as well as George Whitefield, although her Calvinistic theology drew her closer to Whitefield.

Her ministry was to both ends of the social scale, to the high-ranking socialities and to those under the influence of the itinerant preachers. She subsidized these traveling evangelists, built chapels for them (she built over seventy), and spent over half a million dollars. For music in these chapels, she edited hymnbooks, which became very powerful tools in evangelization. She was a friend and patron of Handel, Giardini, who wrote tunes such as "Italian Hymn" for her hymnbook, and Giardano, who also wrote for her hymnal ("Cambridge").

George Whitefield (1714–70)

Whitefield was a great inspirer of hymns, though he wrote none of his own. He will be covered more thoroughly in a study of early American revivals in the next chapter.

John Cennick (1718–55)

John Cennick worked with both John Wesley and George Whitefield. He came into contact with Howell Harris, the Welsh revivalist, joined with him in his outdoor evangelistic tours, and shortly thereafter discovered his own ability to write poetry. By 1741, when he had pledged allegiance to George Whitefield, he had written enough hymns to fill several books. Whitefield liked Cennick's hymns and found them very effective in his meetings. This effectiveness was due in part to a popular practice we have already discussed—antiphonal singing, with the audience or congregation divided in half.

Augustus Toplady (1740–78)

Augustus Toplady was converted at the age of sixteen while attending a Methodist revival. Though he was converted to Methodism, he became convinced through his own study that the Calvinistic position was more biblical than the Arminian position. Caught up in the intense theological temperament of eighteenth-century Christianity, he became a militant supporter of Calvinism.

John Wesley was by now one of the most respected men in England, and the champion of Arminianism, but Toplady frequently battled him by means of pamphlets, sermons, letters, tracts, and hymns. But Bailey points out that Toplady's most famous hymn, "Rock of Ages," was taken from the *Preface* to Wesley's *Hymns on the Lord's Supper*, which had been published thirty years earlier. "Toplady's hymn is Christian plagiarism of the first order!"[17] Despite its origin, "Rock of Ages" has been effective in meeting the needs of many kinds of people of many classes, from Salvation Army meetings to the funeral of Prime Minister Gladstone in Westminster Abbey.

Some of Toplady's hymns have been "Arminianized" by those who are attracted to his hymns but cannot accept his Calvinistic theology.

Eighteenth-Century Welsh Hymnody

Someone has said that the Welsh have never written a bad hymn tune. Whether or not that statement is true, music did play a major role in the Welsh church and revival tradition. Indeed, there was so little Welsh hymn writing before the Welsh revivals that it is safe to say that revival is the true origin of modern Welsh hymnody and what we now call the Welsh hymn tune.

The revival began in 1761 with the preaching of Griffith

---

17. Ibid., p. 120.

Jones. But one of the major personalities of the Welsh revival was William Williams, a Calvinistic Methodist preacher and composer who traveled up and down Wales for forty-three years, covering nearly 96,000 miles and writing eight hundred hymns. He was an excellent preacher, but his greatest influence was through his hymns, most of which were noted for their Bible imagery, for instance, "Guide Me, O Thou Great Jehovah."

The revival practically laid the foundations of musical life in Wales. Around the middle of the century congregational singing became very important. New hymn tunes became widespread through Wesley's and Whitefield's influence on the Welsh revivalists. Instrumental accompaniment was not encouraged, though it was used in certain localities. Numerous folk songs and carols were transformed into hymn tunes, ornamented in each district by local peasants. In their sermons and extempore prayers, Welsh preachers used an emotional semi-chant called the *hwyl,* an intonation similar to many of the folk songs. Congregational expressions eventually led to the now-famous hymn-singing festivals, the *cymanfa ganu.*

Chapter 5

Nineteenth-Century
Evangelical Music

Probably no period of English and American church music history has been more criticized than the nineteenth century. Many serious church musicians today look back on this era with contempt as they view two phenomena: (1) a prevalent church music which was merely a degradation of nineteenth-century secular music; and (2) the advent of the gospel song. These two phenomena had a strong hold, and musicians today with a penchant for sacred art music would be pleased to erase the whole century from the records of church music.

The nineteenth century was a very active period for the amateur church musician. After the classical period ended, the talented secular musician and composer no longer wanted to associate with the music of the church. The influence and domination of the church played a steadily decreasing role in the life of the gifted composer. As a result, fewer composers created totally for the church. Those composers who did write for the church, in trying to emulate the secular Victorian style, actually misused it, and the distinction of church style which had been one of excellence became one of degeneracy. Church music during this period became bad secular music.

One of the important influences in nineteenth-century church music was, according to Erik Routley,

> a rising sophistication of public taste, which called for, and was provided with, hymn tunes in the romantic idiom of Weber and later of Mendelssohn rather than in the classical virtuoso-idiom of Handel. The consequence of this was closer attention to the possibilities of harmony for the sake of its sensational effects, at the expense of florid melody.[1]

A great deal of church music was written during the nineteenth century, but the type of music just mentioned is not the kind of expression that is central to this study. However, with what has been said as background, we shall move more directly into those movements which affected great numbers of Britons in the nineteenth century.

Roots of the Oxford Movement

The social aspect of the Wesleys' work continued in the nineteenth century, but from a different quarter of the Protestant community. Both movements began in Oxford, but the nineteenth-century movement was nothing like the Wesleyan, which began in the low, evangelical church and eventually turned into its own Methodist movement. And, although the Tractarian or Oxford Movement, begun in 1833, had great ramifications for music in the church, there was no accompanying evangelistic fervor as in the former century. Rather, the Oxford Movement saw a return to many of the ideals of the medieval church and its high-church practices.

The greater part of England had not been affected by the surging Methodist evangelical activity. But those who chose to remain with the established church were being robbed of their faith by a largely idle clergy. There have been periods of renewal in the church which have moved in directions other than forward—the Oxford Movement is an example. (The Oxford Movement is, in some ways, similar to the Counter-Reformation of three hundred years earlier.)

---

1. Routley, *The Music of Christian Hymnody*, p. 108.

This movement, in contrast to some renewal movements, was not led by the laity, but was begun and maintained by certain of the clergy. In general, these reformers went back to original sources of musical material. Just as the Council of Trent had attempted to reinstate older musical style, the Oxford Movement tried to move back to sources of hymnody found in the early and medieval church, both east and west. Lay movements tend to utilize folk influences and sources, but *Hymns Ancient and Modern,* the hymnbook of the Oxford reformers, did not. The nonconformist churches had been using a popular style of music; the Oxford Movement was responsible for the return of a more serious musical style in the church. It seemed clear to faithful Anglicans in the nineteenth century, given the rising pressures of a new industrial population and the revolutionary social thinking which had spread from the Continent, that the country would become either totally pagan—or Methodist.

The roots of the Oxford Movement, then, preceded evangelicalism in the nineteenth century, although the evangelical stirrings were present.[2] The Oxford Movement could, in a sense, be considered a countering of the low church movement of John Newton and others who followed in the wake of the Wesleys and Whitefield. Just as the evangelical movement would bring about a new form of sacred music, the Oxford Movement resulted in the rebirth of song, though the songs were ancient—Latin, Greek, and old tunes of the Gregorian tradition. Both movements introduced new music to their respective churches. We see, then, that renewal or revival in the last century is, in certain aspects, similar to the renewal movement of this century. That is, renewal has not been limited to either the liberal or the evangelical fellowships.

In the nineteenth century, the members of the industrial "peasantry" often turned to religion for refuge. Evidence of this idea of Christianity as comfort and solace is found in the Moody-Sankey revivals (see pp. 93ff.) and in the new spirit in the established church. Instead of the music of Methodism, the

---

2. In America and England, this time was also the beginning of the missionary movement.

editors of *Hymns Ancient and Modern* used the tranquil ancient chants.

The new ceremony, the personal holiness attributed to the
ministry, the clergy's new authority as expressed in their vest-
ments, their new title of "Father," along with the use of the
confessional, took some time to be considered by the industrial populace. To those of the lower- and lower-middle
classes, the movement never did become significantly acceptable. However, in its appeal to the intellectual and the educated, the effects of the Oxford Movement have been notable
and lasting.

A few excepts from Routley's *Twentieth Century Church
Music* will point up the differences in hymnody between the
nineteenth-century Oxford Movement and the evangelical
movements:

> If you compare the contents of *Hymns Ancient and Modern*
> (1861) with, say those of *The Psalmist* (1835–43), the most
> successful of the early nineteenth century tunebooks, you will
> find that there is one style which *Ancient and Modern* simply
> will not touch; that is, the florid "Methodist" style with its
> ornamental melody, static bass, occasional fugalities in the
> melody, and repetitions of words.
>
> . . . *Hymns Ancient and Modern* was a firmly bourgeois book
> in that it implied, but never stated, this kind of block criticism
> of a whole style [the Methodist style]. This started something.
> Indeed, it was the beginning of what amounted to virtually a
> century of sociological conflict in church music. And it was
> within a decade that the conflict became more explicit with
> the arrival of the "Gospel-song" style—half music-hall, half
> carol, associated primarily with the evangelistic crusades of
> Dwight L. Moody and Ira D. Sankey.[3]

From the beginning, Moody and Sankey aimed their
evangelistic ministry at those whom the established
churches—Anglican or Dissenting—were not reaching.
There were two results.

> On the one hand, the line of division between those who
> approved and those who abhorred this music was drawn as
> cleanly as was the social line between the class which used it

---

3. Erik Routley, *Twentieth Century Church Music*, pp. 197–98.

and the class which did not. On the other hand, wherever the "established" church (and the orthodox Dissenting churches) felt that they must make an effort to join in the work which the Salvation Army alone was doing with consistent faithfulness, they felt that the music they must use ought to be modelled on the "Sankey" pattern.[4]

Although the strongest influences and movements of revival and renewal were found in England during the nineteenth century, there was some activity on the Continent as well. A good portion of nineteenth-century German church music was thrown open to the popular idiom. And some of the music of the French evangelist, César Malan, was popular in Germany as it was in France.

César Malan (1787–1864) has been called "the Watts and Charles Wesley of French Protestantism."[5] He was the son of religious refugees who had fled France for Geneva. His evangelistic tours took him into many countries on the Continent and in Britain; and wherever he went, in public and in private, "he was a winner of souls."[6] He learned very early the value of sacred song, and many consider him the father of evangelical hymnody in France. He wrote nearly one thousand hymns and in many cases wrote the tunes as well as the texts.

The music of Malan, written under the influence of the Awakening, is simple in its melodic lines and homophonic settings, with clear Romantic tendencies in expressing sentiment.[7]

Special Contributions of America

We must here break into our discussion of the chronological, historical progression and evolution of popularized church music to consider some of the important contribu-

---

4. Ibid.

5. Ninde, *Nineteen Centuries of Christian Song,* p. 78.

6. Ibid.

7. Walter Blankenburg, "Church Music in Reformed Europe," in Friedrich Blume, *Protestant Church Music,* p. 581.

tions of America toward the spread of the gospel through "the music of the people."

Early America closely followed the example of England in using metrical Psalms in early worship services. The Psalms were followed, in the eighteenth century, by the hymns of Watts and Wesley. By the nineteenth century, the songs of the camp meetings and Sunday school were used, which were greatly influenced by Negro spirituals and the minstrel music of the time. All of this was important background for the most significant idiom of the nineteenth century—the gospel song of Ira D. Sankey. (This will receive more attention at the end of this chapter.)

The *singing school movement* was influential in many of the colonial areas of early America, particularly in rural sections. Many churches had one-day singing schools, which frequently met every fifth Sunday. Great preparation was made for these sessions and a great deal of practicing was done. The singing school was an important factor in the spread of the gospel and revival hymns.

The earliest worship materials in America were the Psalters and the hymns imported from England. In America, as in England, there was before long a movement from the Psalms to hymns. In 1729, Benjamin Franklin published some of Isaac Watts's evangelical hymns. These were further popularized in the colonies through the visits of revivalist George Whitefield in 1739 and 1740.

George Whitefield, along with Jonathan Edwards, was an important personality in "the Great Awakening" of 1740–45. Music played a vital role in this period of revival. Early in the Awakening the wide use of singing, particularly the singing of groups of young people along the streets of the cities and roads of the countryside, had a profound effect on the population. In the Great Awakening "thousands of nominal Christians were caught up in evangelistic fervor that shattered old forms and traditions and opened new channels of spiritual growth for entire congregations."[8]

Whitefield, an Anglican clergyman, toured the New En-

---

8. David Poling, "Religion in America," *Scranton Times* (Pa.), March 3, 1976.

gland colonies preaching a somewhat modified version of the old authoritarian Calvinism. Each individual was given some measure of responsibility for his own salvation and some responsibility in the salvation of his neighbor.

> Along with this new democratic faith there arose a desire for a more personal musical expression. . . . The revival converts of George Whitefield, Gilbert Tennent, and Jonathan Edwards required a musical expression emphasizing the relationship between Christ and the individual, a theme not present in the metrical psalms.[9]

The eventual musical compromise was to be found in the Isaac Watts *Imitations of the Psalms of David*. This evangelical enthusiasm, combined with the Calvinistic retention of serious self-discipline in sacred music forms, had other musical implications. In a study of colonial religious music, Covey wrote:

> The result was a liberalized and vitalized Calvinistic music, but not the extremely unrestrained singing that we associate with the later camp-meeting or the "free-will" sects.[10]

Covey also said:

> The distinction between himself [Whitefield] and John Wesley . . . is observable in his music view. . . . Whitefield was no singing evangelist, never a propagandist of the Methodist hymnody, but preferred a sober strain of song, greatly admiring Watts' *Psalms and Hymns*. He took a Wesley hymnal or so along and had one of them reprinted in America; he even adopted some of the Wesley hymns in his own hymnal; but he was not an unqualified Wesleyan hymnist. . . . His preferential regard for Watts is seen in his carrying on his tours a copy of Watts' *Psalms and Hymns* bound up with the Anglican prayer-book; [and] in the predominance of Watts over the Wesleys in the hymnbook he compiled.[11]

Like Wesley, however, Whitefield encouraged social hymn-singing, and wherever Whitefield went he stimulated

---

9. James C. Downey, "The Great Awakening and the Music of the Baptists, 1740–1800," pp. 20–27.

10. Cyclone Covey, "Religion and Music in Colonial America," p. 113.

11. Ibid., p. 114.

the movement from psalmody to hymnody. A number of the preachers associated with Whitefield became hymn writers. Of the music of Whitefield's revivals, it has been said, in retrospect, that his preference for the hymns of Watts "would prove far to the right compared to the almost savage-rendered folk-hymnody of those evangelical sects unchecked by a Calvinistic view of redemption."[12]

According to James Downey, the increased personalization of the song material of the Great Awakening can be seen in the music used by Jonathan Edwards. Downey states:

> The transformation from metrical psalmody to evangelical hymnody was a change in the function of music from a sacred duty performed within the framework of a worship service into a highly personal, spontaneous statement of religious feeling. The two functions were not mutually exclusive, but in 1741 when the revival which Edwards and others had encouraged appeared to be on the verge of destroying their religious institutions, singing in the streets was one part of the revival which could be sacrificed in the interest of peace and harmony.[13]

Methodism in Early America

The Methodist Episcopal Church in America was organized in Baltimore in 1784. At that time the liturgy and order of worship devised by John Wesley for the new American church was adopted. Methodists did not use the formal orders of service very long, however, for they soon became involved in their pioneer evangelistic work. Formal worship fit the Methodists' religious and social needs less and less in those days. Rarely were the services held in a church building. The preachers adapted their preaching and singing to the spirit and need of the people to whom they ministered.

Louis Benson feels that the Methodists' dominance in the early American camp meeting was due largely to their hymns and vital hymn singing. Benson explains that hymnbooks were so scarce that existing hymnals were cut apart and the

---

12. Ibid., p. 116.

13. James Downey, "The Music of American Revivalism, 1740–1800," p. 24.

pages distributed so that all the people might learn the hymns. Soon, however, these hymns did not express the intense feelings of preacher and people. As a result, spontaneous songs began to arise; they became a distinctive characteristic of the meetings.[14]

> Rough and irregular couplets or stanzas were concocted out of Scripture phrases and everyday speech with liberal interspersing of Hallelujahs and refrains. Such ejaculatory hymns were frequently started by an excited auditor during the preaching, and taken up by the throng until the meeting dissolved in singing—ecstasy, culminating in a general hand shaking. Sometimes they were given forth by a preacher who had a sense of rhythm, under the excitement of his preaching and the agitation of his audience.[15]

Some of these early rough songs were written down and printed, although most were not and have perished. The first camp meeting song books come from the beginning of the nineteenth century, and no doubt contain the best of the repertoire. With these songs, a second phase of camp meeting hymnody developed in which there were "song writers who paid more attention to the rules of rhetoric and versification and whose work, therefore, had greater claim to permanence."[16]

According to Benson's description, this type of song was very much like the revival hymn of the 1920s, but it was more crude since it reflected the language and phraseology of the primitive life of the people. The only stylistic requirement for a tune was that it be contagious and effective.

Although most early American hymnody was a product or a by-product of England, before long the warmth of black music made itself felt. The first indigenous American hymn is also largely a product of the black man.

> The "negro spiritual" was born of the Kentucky Revivals of 1797–1805 consequent on the evangelisation of the negroes,

---

14. Louis F. Benson, *The English Hymn: Its Development and Use in Worship*, p. 292.

15. Ibid.

16. Ibid.

and of their great sufferings in the days of slavery. They were evangelised just early enough for their sufferings to be expressed in this sublime and primitive music.[17]

American Folk Hymnody, Spirituals, and Early Gospel Hymns

In indigenous American music, the tunes are the most important consideration, since many of the texts are European—generally from Watts, the Wesleys, or John Newton (there are some anonymous writers).[18] The folk hymns were an integral part of Protestant evangelical activity, which followed the example set by John Wesley in England and America. The tunes came from Tennessee, Kentucky, the Carolinas, Virginia, and the Cumberland Gap area; they offered a musical freedom "far beyond the 'allowed' tunes . . . of the authorities until religious gatherings were musically completely liberated."[19] Hundreds of folk hymns were created which had music and text that "spoke from the heart of the devout in the language of the common man."[20]

Many of the folk hymn tunes show a strange dichotomy. They are either ruggedly powerful (e.g., "Volunteers," No. 70; "Albion," No. 78; "Land of Rest," No. 81), or sentimental (e.g., "Tribulation," No. 69; "Rest in Heaven," No. 73; "I Love Thee," No. 134).[21] The folk hymns used in camp meetings usually followed a traditional folk form—stanza with refrain. William Reynolds describes the typical folk hymn form:

> Sometimes an existing hymn text was used with an added refrain, such as "On Jordan's stormy banks I stand" and "At the cross." Frequently the text was simplified with a recurring line interspersed between the lines of the hymn text, such as

17. Routley, *The Music of Christian Hymnody*, p. 165.

18. Until recently, the field of American folk hymnody was largely neglected except for the studies made by George Pullen Jackson and Annabel Morris Buchanan.

19. George Pullen Jackson, *Spiritual Folk-Songs of Early America,* p. 6.

20. Ibid.

21. Examples selected from Jackson, *Spiritual Folk-Songs.*

"Blessed be the name." Other songs took the form of de-
tached "choruses." These used one line repeated three times
with an added fourth line. Additional stanzas kept the same
pattern with slight variation.[22]

In the years of American slavery, a strong evangelical
movement began among the blacks (1797–1805). The music
which resulted had great influence on (and indeed was an
important part of) American folk hymody. These songs were
known as Negro spirituals—expressive hymns full of nostal-
gic longing, particularly for release from pain ("Nobody
Knows the Trouble I've Seen" and "Deep River").

Early in the nineteenth century the slavery question was
weighing on the conscience of some Americans. This was a
time of great prosperity in the United States, however, and
most Americans were determined to gather riches. The ma-
terialistic emphasis caused religious life to decline until the
middle of the century, when there was the almost inevitable
economic crash. In such conditions, a fall in the economy and
the threat of war, men are compelled to turn to God, and
revival becomes possible.[23]

A vast revival did occur in the United States and Canada,
followed by the greatest European revival in history which
swept through Great Britain and into the Continent. At first,
the American revivals used existing hymnals; the old, familiar
texts took on new meaning. Soon, however, the limitations of
old hymnbooks became apparent, and new hymns were produced in great abundance. These new hymns represented,
says Bailey,

> a new emphasis in religion. The essence of it consisted in
> cultivating the mystic, personal side: communion with God,
> fervent love of Christ as God, contemplation of heaven as the
> reward for the faithful endurance of the ills of life, nature as
> an approach to God, the winning of souls through conversion
> rather than through baptism, the spread of the Gospel to all
> lands.[24]

---

22. William J. Reynolds, "Folk Element in American Church Music," p. 3.

23. Cecil J. Allen, *Hymns and the Christian Faith*, p. 104.

24. Bailey, *The Gospel in Hymns,* p. 482.

In the 1870s, a great number of what became known as "gospel hymns" were added to the American church music. This was a distinctly American phenomenon, developing out of the earlier decades of the century. The songs were evangelical in spirit, focusing on the winning of souls through conversion. Though these songs were primarily used in revivals, they were also popular in Sunday schools, Christian associations, and in many churches made up of less educated members. To these, literary form and quality had much less appeal than did emotional content.

Some of the hymn collections of the late nineteenth century combined the new gospel hymns with the earlier hymns that were in general use. One of the major collections was the *Soldiers' Hymn Book,* which was greatly used in the Civil War, accounting for the use of military metaphors in many of the hymns. These gospel hymns gave evangelists of the postwar revival the musical material they needed.[25]

A significant part of the leadership of late nineteenth-century American revival was the Young Men's Christian Association, the Y.M.C.A. This organization was founded in London in 1844 and was operating in Montreal and Boston by 1851. The Y.M.C.A. played a major role in the revival that swept through the larger American cities and helped to popularize the gospel hymn.

> During the Civil War the "Y" carried these hymns into the army and the *Soldier's Hymn Book* became a leading instrument of army work.... After the war the "Y" began a large revival work in the cities of the north and soon adopted the Gospel hymn as its distinctive type. These hymns gave to the evangelists of the postwar revival exactly the aid needed for their campaigns.[26]

Dwight L. Moody was made President of the Chicago Y.M.C.A. in 1865. In 1870 he was joined by a Y.M.C.A. secretary, Ira D. Sankey. As a team they were to make history in evangelism and evangelistic music.

---

25. Allen, *Hymns and the Christian Faith,* pp. 105–106.
26. Bailey, *The Gospel in Hymns,* p. 483.

The Gospel Song: Background and Description

The gospel song is one of the most important parts of the sacred song heritage of evangelicals. A concise definition of this form is somewhat difficult. However, there is sufficient similarity among most of the songs of this style to be able to give a general description. They are subjective songs emphasizing human experience and testimony. Frequently these songs press for a decision on the part of the listener. The music is normally simple, easily sung and easily learned, with simple harmony and lilting rhythm. In form it is free; in character it is emotional; in purpose and spirit it is evangelistic. The songs usually develop a single thought, which generally culminates after each verse with a chorus or refrain bringing unity to all of the stanzas. It could be said that the gospel song is a compromise between the hymn and the Negro spiritual, and it combines the function of song and homily. It is addressed to the people rather than to God. Supporting this view, Hustad states,

> The genius of gospel music is its simplicity—its artless rhyming and its simple, almost amateurish music. There is an unmistakable kinship between emotional expression and our traditional concept of Christian experience.[27]

Gospel music and mass evangelism (as we have come to know them during the last one hundred years) began with the urban crusades of Dwight L. Moody (1837–99). Music, both from the audience and from performers on the platform (usually by his music director, Ira Sankey, 1840–1908), played a very important part in his crusades, particularly as a means of preparation for Moody's sermons. It has been said of Moody that he could not sing a note, and that his interest in music was based largely on the ability of the music to condition the crowd—a utilitarian view of music, to be sure.[28]

27. Donald Hustad, "Problems in Psychology and Aesthetics in Music."
28. Robert Stevenson, *Patterns in Protestant Church Music,* pp. 155, 160–61.

Effects of Gospel Song in
the Nineteenth Century

The music which Sankey and Moody found to be the most effective was what was later called the "gospel song." These men began their association for the cause of evangelism in 1870, and in 1872 began their first evangelistic campaign in England. In 1874, Philip Bliss, preparing for his musical ministry with evangelist D. W. Whittle, published a small collection of sacred songs using the title *Gospel Songs*. Benson explains that in 1875, upon the return of Moody and Sankey from England,

> it was decided to unite the Sacred Songs and Solos [a sixteen-page pamphlet used by Sankey]... with materials furnished by Bliss' book, and the joint collection was published as *Gospel Hymns and Sacred Songs* by P. P. Bliss and Ira D. Sankey, as used by them in gospel meetings.[29]

The ministry of the gospel song was thus launched. Several more editions followed and became extremely popular. Benson goes on to say:

> The Gospel Hymns may be said to have carried the emotional and less cultivated element of religious people off its feet, and to have furnished for a time the familiar songs of vast numbers hitherto unacquainted with hymns and unused to public worship. The new melodies penetrated even the music halls and were whistled by the man on the street.[30]

Although the names of Moody and Sankey must be linked with the gospel song, they actually only utilized established musical practices, blending them to create a popular sacred song. The music and the idea of popularized singing was not new. What was distinctive was the tremendous success this preacher-musician team achieved.

The gospel song also had deep roots in the folk hymnody of this country, in the songs of the camp meeting, and the religious song of the Sunday school. By the middle of the

---

29. Benson, *The English Hymn,* pp. 486–87.
30. Ibid.

nineteenth century the Sunday school movement was becoming a significant evangelical force. Generally, the important songs of this movement were simple ones, written to help children learn Scriptural truths. All of these related song forms were influential predecessors of the gospel song, and are more historical examples of the lighter sacred popular song that has remained at the border of church worship. Harry Eskew states:

> As the camp-meeting hymn was the musical expression of the rural revivalism of the early nineteenth century, so in the latter half of the century the gospel hymn was the musical expression of urban revivalism.[31]

Much of the revival movement of the nineteenth century, particularly that which is associated with Moody and Sankey in the last twenty-five years, says Routley, ministered particularly to the

> dispossessed and outcast on the collective principle. Mass-meetings and mass-salvation are the mainstays of the revivalist technique, and the revivals of the nineteenth century brought the gospel to many to whom the Bible was a closed book and the Church a barred mansion. One of the distinguishing marks of Revivalist technique is the emphasis in its preaching on judgment, together with the emphasis in the singing on peace. And singing played, on the whole, a greater part than preaching, certainly a greater part than reason, in the success of the movement.[32]

Moody's and Sankey's revival techniques came from America, where for about a century after the Kentucky Revivals of the late eighteenth century the means for encouraging revival were well known and practiced. The familiar music of these Kentucky revivals, mostly Negro spirituals, had done much to bring about the success of the revivals held by Moody and Sankey.

Moody and Sankey also sought to use a folk style in their revival music when they went to England. However, the in-

---

31. Harry Eskew, "Music in the Baptist Tradition," p. 171.
32. Routley, *The Church and Music,* p. 187.

dustrial revolution had meant the dispossession of the common people, which had meant also the dispossession of much of their music. So Sankey composed and adapted music which he felt would appeal to the listeners.

Despite the fact that some gospel songs are of poor quality, no body of music can be simply cast away as unworthy. Any music deserves to be considered on the merits of each individual piece. The gospel song can be regarded as symbolic of a music designed for homeless people. The people to whom Moody and Sankey ministered responded to music which gave them a feeling of hope, sometimes with a minimum of effort.

Commercialism

Nearly everything which is worthy and good eventually becomes a marketable product. History reveals that the making and selling of gospel songs soon grew into a huge enterprise, and the production of these songs became a great commercial venture.[33]

One company used the following advertisement in promoting one of their gospel song books:

> Songs that have reaped the greatest results for the most experienced evangelists and singers in the evangelistic field. Songs that received the greatest number of votes in the recent contest. Eleven new songs that present the old, old message in a new way that is effective, appealing and forceful, together with favorite old standard hymns. . . . Nothing better in its line to be had.[34]

According to Stevenson, the publishers were more interested in the financial income than the religious results. This was increasingly seen as publishers collected a large number of copyrights on popular, secular songs and patterned their gospel songs after these secular songs.

There is no way to determine the exact number of songs that were written in the gospel idiom, but estimates run into

---

33. Stevenson, *The Story of Southern Hymnology,* p. 72.
34. Ibid., p. 83.

the tens of thousands. Fanny Crosby herself is said to have written approximately eight thousand song texts.

Detractors of the Gospel Song

The gospel song, like most other forms of church music, has had its critics as well as its supporters. Cecil Allen has written:

> The crudity of the music ... lies in the almost complete lack of inventiveness in so many of the tunes. Some throughout their length consist of no more than three or four chords or their inversions, with endless repetitions of musical phrases.[35]

Allen goes on to say that even though it is sometimes claimed that this is a necessary kind of simplicity, in many cases the simplicity degenerates into deadly monotony.

One of the chief American antagonists of the gospel song was Dr. H. M. Poteat, professor of Latin at Wake Forest College in North Carolina. In 1921 he produced a book entitled *Practical Hymnology.* Chapter two, "The Cheap Hymn," is one of the most scathing attacks upon the recent revival hymn that has ever appeared. In this chapter, Poteat maintains that the chief reason for the tremendous popularity of the gospel "hymn" is the popular fondness for secular music of the same type which was characteristic of the time.

> Blues, jazz, waltzes, ragtime, slushy sentimentality have become the musical expression of so many people outside the church, that the same sort of thing, with a poor, thin veneer of religion, is demanded in the church.[36]

In Defense of the Gospel Song

Although many have criticized the music of the Sankey style, some respected church musicians have defended it. Erik Routley writes:

> Some of us have poked fun at the trite jingles of the Sankey revival. But trapped miners have sung "Hold the Fort!" and

---

35. Allen, *Hymns and the Christian Faith,* p. 108.
36. Cited in Stevenson, *The Story of Southern Hymnology,* pp. 86–87.

who knows how many people have calmed elemental fears of death with "Shall We Gather at the River?" and beaten off the gnawing fear of hunger and insecurity and dispossession with "Will Your Anchor Hold?"[37]

The distinguished hymnologist Louis Benson agrees that all gospel songs should not be considered as a group when determining their value. He stated that "gospel songs are not a homogenous mass, and they should be judged like other hymns upon their individual merit."[38]

Donald Hustad has made several valid points of rebuttal to some of the more common criticisms of the gospel song. A list of these criticisms follows, each one accompanied with a summary of his response.

1. *Gospel songs are too simple, too repetitious.* The strength of the gospel song is its simplicity, artlessness, and repetition. To desire that the average worshiper's understanding be increased does not change the fact that theological comprehension is approximately that of a twelve-year-old.

2. *Gospel songs are too personal and selfish.* Evangelicals (including Martin Luther) claim that the essense of salvation is the personal pronoun.

3. *Gospel songs center more on personal experience than on Christ.* While the truly worthy gospel songs will emphasize the centrality of Christ in the Christian experience, the person who has experienced salvation must have a song to express the way he feels.

4. *Gospel songs are anthropomorphic.* But this is what Christ came to be—God in the flesh. The God who created the universe is also a close Friend. Both of these truths must be represented in sacred song.

5. *Gospel songs are too sentimental.* Although this may be true of some songs, the Christian is not to be robbed of a proper emotional response to God's truth. Without emotion the human will does not respond. And one must realize that

---

37. Erik Routley, *Hymns and Human Life,* p. 7.
38. Benson, *The English Hymn,* p. 491.

an individual's emotional response frequently depends on his culture.[39]

Debasement of a Style

The original gospel songs had a distinct quality that set them apart from some of the imitations that followed Sankey. The strength of the "vintage" song of Sankey was the melody. His tunes were simple—easily and quickly learned—and did not depend on the harmonic color that was so typical of the art music of the time. The harmony was usually confined to the three primary chords: tonic, dominant, and subdominant.

The best tunes of Sankey have an unassuming simplicity that results from the absence of musical tension. The later use of exaggerated rhythms and chromatic harmony contributed to a degradation of the simple Sankey style. None of the hymns of Sankey can be charged with gaudiness or flamboyance.

Whether we study the gospel song of the late nineteenth century or witness music of any other age, we must decide if the borrowed material used to put the song into the marketplace is secular merely in style or thoroughly pagan. For many agree that putting sacred or religious words to music does not immediately cause that music to be sacrosanct. To some degree, the function of words and music is separate and distinct.

According to one writer, some church musicians maintain that

the more beautiful a melody is from the sensuous point of view the less desirable it is as a hymn melody. This is where most of the gospel hymn melodies are guilty—they are too sensuous. The gospel hymn melodies call too much attention to themselves and not enough to the text. They are, to use Canon Douglas' expression, "manward and not Godward. . . ." This hymnization of the gospel hymn is only a reflection of the spiritual state of the evangelical church. The problem

---

39. Based on Donald Hustad, "Spiritual Music for a Spiritual Church," p. 11.

which besets us is whether the Church can learn from the world and still preserve the traditional spirit and dignity of her music. The history of church art, particularly of church music, is the history of the conflict between the sacerdotal conception of art and the popular taste. It is a fallacy to assert that the masses of the people are responsive only to that which is trivial and sensational.[40]

Conclusion

The gospel song of the late nineteenth century is certainly one of the most important examples of a popular religious expression, but it was not a new idea. Gospel music will continue to exist and have an appeal because it meets the needs of certain people. The music evangelist before and after Ira Sankey has recognized that there is a place for this kind of "transient" expression. But when this artless, disposable music becomes "classic," the persistent user will begin to have difficulty. If this music increasingly finds its way into the worship service, it soon becomes overused. John Lilley explains:

> A continuing problem inherent in the manner of religious expression centers around the historical fact of "use malaise." The truly popular expressions of any period, whatever the medium, become anachronistic through their excessive use. They are so repeated that they become meaningless, rote ceremonies, following a formula rather than an inspirational guide.
> An example of this "use malaise" is readily apparent in the gospel song. It is reflective of a particular culture which existed in the late 19th century, but as the 20th century progressed it became increasingly irrelevant to the style and understandings of the new age.[41]

The gospel song was tremendously popular in the last years of the nineteenth century. Through the commercialization of these songs and later imitations, the style was propagated in the twentieth century. As a result, many of these songs have

---

40. Lee Olson, "Church Music and Secularism," p. 10.
41. Lilley, "New Principles of Worship," p. 13.

become better known in this century than they were in the last, even though the sound is growing more out of date. Nevertheless, many people today are very fond of some of these songs. For some of them this fondness is based on an emotional or sentimental association, but it is a strong feeling, nevertheless. To many, these are *the* songs of witness. And so, the church musician must learn to balance his role between artist and minister. If a sincere minister of music loves his people, he will not ignore any of them.

Lilley goes on to say,

> One solution to the problem of making a living tradition liveable may lie in the use of the best of the past in terms which are meaningful and fulfilling to those of the present. The contributions of the late 19th century, or any other period for that matter, must be adapted so that the needs of present cultural subgroups are met. The historical thread of the contribution, however, must remain visible.[42]

Church music of any period is dependent in varying degrees on its musical traditions. It is easy to say that our century was probably more influenced by evangelical developments of the previous century than any other era in history. This, however, would be difficult to prove.

From our brief survey of the gospel song movement, we turn to examine the music which has been used for church outreach in the twentieth century. We will deal with the revolution in church music as it accompanied church renewal and revival of the sixties and seventies.

---

42. Ibid., p. 14.

Chapter 6

Music of Evangelism:
1900–1960

Roots of the Gospel Song

The evangelical religious temper of the twentieth century is in many ways directly influenced by the developments of the nineteenth century. A great deal of the evangelical music of the twentieth century has roots in the gospel song tradition of Ira Sankey. Indeed, by the turn of the century, gospel music began to override all other forms of sacred music. This new form emerged after a century of Protestant reformation, the missionary movement, and the free church movement in which the church was not bound by the authority of bishops.

In the evangelical church there was an almost complete disregard for the historic hymn, the official song of the church. The laity strongly influenced musical trends away from the great song tradition. This is not to the credit of evangelicals, and caused much musical weakness during the early generations of this century. The trend in the first half of the twentieth century was toward debasement of the classical revivalist idiom through use of rhythmic mannerisms and chromatic harmony.

Even the music used by Billy Graham, one of the most

popular contemporary evangelists, "has largely depended on materials developed since 1850, borrowing some items from each period."[1]

This trend was observed in the early years of this century, as Benson wrote:

> The Revival Influence was the first to affect the Hymnody, and has affected it in the same way from the eighteenth century Revival to the latest [1915] evangelism. The Methodist Movement modified the ideal of the Hymn, and created the Evangelistic Hymn, and each succeeding revival movement has turned from the established Church Hymnody and created an independent body of Spiritual Song with a fresher warmth and an immediate appeal to popular taste.[2]

The music of Ira Sankey was such an important influence that even today his name is spoken together with the name of Dwight Moody. Sankey's style of music, along with the missionary activity in the evangelical church, has resulted, according to Donald Hustad, in "one of the most astounding cultural transfers in all history. Anglo-American gospel songs have, wisely or unwisely, been translated into every language in which the Word of God is preached."[3]

In certain contexts, it is apparent that some of the Sankey-type songs have been, and still could be, appropriately used. In some cases, effective words have been enhanced by a change in the musical setting. Cecil Allen points out that "the indifferent harmonizations of airs which in themselves are acceptable have been altered to their advantage."[4]

The subject of many texts of the early twentieth-century revival hymns was to forcibly direct attention to the danger of eternal destruction. However, most of the texts and tunes were written in archaic language. Preston Rockholt writes

---

1. Hustad, "Music and the Church's Outreach," p. 182. For further information, see: George Stansbury, "The Music of the Billy Graham Crusades, 1947–1970."

2. Benson, *The English Hymn*, p. 567.

3. Donald Hustad, lecture given at the Billy Graham School of Evangelism, New York City, June, 1969.

4. Allen, *Hymns and the Christian Faith*, p. 109.

concerning this continuing use of the gospel music of an earlier period:

> Let us not confuse what is timeless with what was written in great haste to be used by certain people in special circumstances as disposable music—disposable except that a publisher got ahold [*sic*] of it. . . .
> Bliss, Lowry, Stebbins, Sankey and Rodeheaver were used of God greatly in evangelical church music a century and much less ago. What a mistake it is to base our technique upon their work now. God has called us to a new hour and opportunity. His work cannot be reduced to any single style or technique. Jesus said that the winds of God blow where they will, and history would tell us that God's spirit blows most often in new forms and new techniques. . . . We surely can observe, though, that where true spiritual awakening has come about there has been an outburst of new hymnody, new service patterns, new voices, new methods, new literature.[5]

Church music styles of the twentieth century have preserved more of their nineteenth-century heritage than has secular music. In this way, continuity is preserved to a greater degree inside the church than outside. This is largely due to the fact that the church is traditionally wary of human inventions.

In viewing the social conditions of America between 1865 and 1900, most historians agree that there had never before in our history been a period of such revolutionary change. Indeed, obvious parallels can be drawn between those years and the twenty-five years beginning around 1950. Both were times of innovation and industrial or technological development. Both were times of political, moral, and religious chaos. The gospel music of these two periods offered some satisfaction for the needs of the time. And, there is an inescapable association between the satisfactions offered in the gospel songs and the deficiencies of the period.[6]

Is church music history repeating itself for a present revolutionary purpose? Today's witness music has turned from

---

5. Preston Rockholt, "Creative Tensions in Church Music."

6. For further information, see Charles Hulrich Zwingli Meyer, "Sacred Lyrics of Protestant America: A Sociological Study in Compensation," p. 165.

earlier traditions toward a closer involvement with society, and, as with the music of the late nineteenth century, is giving more attention to personal needs. In this respect, much of the history of church music can be evaluated in the light of social anthropology. Music, both for the secular world and for the church, has always been a reflection of the outlook and needs of the people of that generation.

Billy Sunday and Homer Rodeheaver

The next nationally renowned voice of mass evangelism after Moody and Sankey was the team of Billy Sunday and Homer Rodeheaver. Music and singing always played an important part in the meetings of Billy Sunday, who was a converted baseball player. As one of Sunday's biographers, William Ellis, reports:

> Mr. Sunday set the city to singing. His sermons were framed in music—not music that was a performance by some soloist, but music that ministered to his message. His gospel was sung as well as preached. The singing was as essential a part of the service as the sermon. Everybody likes good music, especially of a popular sort. Sunday saw that this taste was gratified.[7]

Ellis wrote that there was less "religious ragtime" in the Sunday meetings than one might expect in revival meetings of this type.

Homer Rodeheaver used many devices to impress the crowds with the music. Sometimes he directed the music to produce an antiphonal effect between the choir and the audience. Whatever the technique, the audience was always given plenty of opportunity to share in the music of the meetings, and sometimes was even given an opportunity to select favorite songs or hymns. Occasionally delegations were allowed to stand and sing a song of their choice. In support of this, Ellis writes,

> It was no valid objection to the Sunday music that it was so thoroughly entertaining. The tabernacle crowds sang, not as a

---

7. William Ellis, *Billy Sunday: The Man and His Message,* pp. 119–20.

religious duty, but for the sheer joy of singing. . . . The echoes of tabernacle music could be heard long after Mr. Sunday had gone from a community.[8]

Billy Sunday and Homer Rodeheaver were much more interested in entertaining their audience than were most evangelistic teams before or after them. Donald Hustad even calls Rodeheaver "a jokester, an entertainer pure and simple."[9]

Evangelical music of witness and Christian experience in the first half of this century tended to reflect the secular idiom of the day, whether it was the era of swing or the big band. At times, some of the styles emulated the songs of the nightclub. Whether these were conscious or subconscious imitations is hard to say, for most composers to some degree imitate the music upon which they have fed. It is interesting to note that shortly after female trios and quartets (such as the McGuire Sisters and the Chordettes) became popular on secular radio in the fifties, music specially arranged for similar groups was heard in many evangelical circles.

Music of Billy Graham Crusades of the 1950s

In his discussion of the music in the crusades of Billy Graham, George Stansbury maintains that the music continued the tradition already quite familiar from the crusade music of Moody-Sankey and Sunday-Rodeheaver. Stansbury claims that nothing particularly new or creative was offered by the Graham musicians. Erik Routley, writing about the Graham meetings in London during the 1950s, said:

> But I contend that the evangelism of Martin Luther was not associated with anything like this kind of music, nor was that of John Wesley. . . . If Dr. Graham means business when he says he wants not to found a new sect but to send his young penitents back to the churches, this sort of music will not help

---

8. Ibid., p. 122.

9. Interview with Donald Hustad, Southern Baptist Theological Seminary, Louisville, Kentucky, April 14, 1977.

him because they won't be hearing it in their own churches. ...Why then did not Dr. Graham prepare them through the use of familiar and great hymns for what they will, as he claims to hope, meet in the churches?...It cannot be argued that the Gospel songs were familiar to the mass of the people there. No hymns are familiar to the people Dr. Graham wants to convert. He was not letting them sing what they knew, but teaching them what they would always associate in after years with his campaign. Does this support his argument that the object of the campaign was to bring people back to the churches?... The people who attend Graham meetings will love and remember anything that they hear there. Why give them this stuff?[10]

Routley raises the vital issue of the relationship of church music to modern evangelism, and also the problem of the artistic chasm between the "highbrow" and the "plain man."

Musical Evangelism in Smaller Settings

In addition to the sort of mass evangelism through crusades attempted by Billy Graham, there are several organizations that, though they have nationwide ministries, work in smaller, less imposing settings on a local level. One of these organizations is Youth for Christ (Y.F.C.), an interdenominational organization specializing in teenage evangelism. Since its founding in 1944, local Y.F.C. organizations have sponsored rallies, contests, and camps, and music has always been an important part of this ministry.

In many Y.F.C. rallies both sacred and secular music is used in order to attract the teenagers, and to carry the gospel message. In his extensive study of music in the Youth for Christ program, Robert Horner states:

Sacred music far outweighs the secular music in most rallies. Some rally directors bitterly oppose the use of secular music and others equally firmly believe that secular music is an effective bridge to the non-Christian teenager or that the barrier between sacred and secular is an artificial one.[11]

---

10. Erik Routley, "On the Billy Graham Songbook," p. 26.

11. Robert B. Horner, "The Function of Music in the Youth for Christ Program," p. 12.

Two groups with an active ministry in musical evangelism on college campuses are InterVarsity and Campus Crusade for Christ. Music is generally a regular part of the evangelistic technique used in the campus meetings. Many local chapters have their own well-rehearsed musical groups which perform for the local meetings, and both have had professional musical groups traveling from campus to campus in the United States and in foreign countries. In addition, Campus Crusade has sponsored summer training sessions at their headquarters in California for singing groups desiring a ministry in musical evangelism.

In recent years both of these organizations have featured a style of music which can be described as "sacred folk" or "sacred folk-rock." A generation ago InterVarsity showed good balance in its musical selectivity by introducing some of the fine, serious hymnody of the English Keswick tradition in its *Hymnal.* Even InterVarsity's new hymnal, *Hymns II,* is quite conservative, though it does have a number of contemporary folk-style songs from the evangelical-Anglican tradition.

The Struggling Church at Mid-Century

There are several curiosities of the mid-twentieth century church to be discussed. It is an established fact that many denominations were struggling at this time; national polls as well as denominational statistics indicated a loss in attendance and membership. This fact, along with the knowledge that population was rapidly increasing, caused church leaders extreme concern.

This problem was discussed in great depth in an attempt to determine what the problems were, who or what was at fault, or what techniques had outlived their usefulness. (In some areas, this concern became the grassroots movement for church renewal.) There were a number of recommendations, some leading to the techniques used in the past decade. In many of the church ministries, healthy new approaches have been used successfully, for most churches acknowledge that though the gospel and biblical truths do not change, the means of presenting them do.

In the field of music, however, it has nearly always been the case that the church has seen the need for change *after* non-sacred music is far ahead. In the mid-twentieth century, much of the musical practice of the evangelical church was steeped in the traditions of the late nineteenth and early twentieth century gospel songs and hymns. This tradition was very hard to shake, since it was one of the most popular and far-reaching styles the evangelical church had ever known. The wide use of the gospel song along with the millions of printed copies of gospel hymnals and hymns caused its roots to penetrate deeply into evangelical church music tradition.

Even today this old, often worn-out idiom of the gospel song is the music which the older, more mature members of the church love and to which they respond. The majority of these people feel that this is the music which "does the job." That is, it creates a warm, sometimes sentimental feeling because of the long association the songs have had with the people's Christian past. Such church members assume that even today this music can speak out in witness and testimony to those outside the church. The great problem, however, is that this music has not been speaking to non-Christians.

In the mid-twentieth century, non-Christians in the church service were already becoming increasingly rare. As a result, most of these songs were being sung in church by the older, faithful members; they were singing to themselves. Even young people within the church had difficulty relating their Christian experience to the frequently archaic lyrics and musical idioms. If the youth were to be retained as the future of the church, something had to be done to provide them with a valid and appropriate expression of their testimony and witness.

Although ministers of music acknowledged the facts and the problems, very little was done for many years. The church simply did not have any new music. This lack of creativity was an indication that the church was not spiritually healthy.

Some Musical Consequences
of Church Renewal

Periods of renewal in the church's history have always been accompanied by an outburst of new Christian song. Generally the musical style for that song has been taken from outside the church. The church's attempts to find new language for worship and outreach have resulted in numerous new translations of Scripture and new music.

Into a musical vacuum came the young Christians' answer, with what many called inappropriate experience and witness music. Their music came in the form of folk, pop, and rock styles which were clear emulations of the secular pop music scene. Older, more mature evangelicals were predictably horrified, but the idioms were in existence and growing in use. From all appearances these new styles were going to be around for some time, not passing away as a brief experiment, as some had hoped. The young people had a musical style with which to witness, one which was already quite developed.

In the initial stages of this new music, years of musical training were not necessary in order to produce a convincing sound. One could at least say that it was loud. The 1960s ushered in the age of the guitar, in which a few simple chords and amplification equipment combined to emphasize rhythm and a heavy beat. Gospel folk and gospel rock groups began in England in the early 1960s and the craze spread quickly to the United States.

By the 1970s, nearly every country with some evangelical Christian witness was forced to take a position on the use of the new sacred music. Revival in most fellowships of the Christian church was widely felt to be long overdue, and the traditional music of the church was found just as wanting as any of the other methods of ministry.

A "Solution" from England

Having briefly viewed the need of the church at mid-century, we will now look at the phenomenon of the new church music at its inception and development.

The churches of America were having difficulty attracting people, but the churches of England confronted even deeper problems. Many of the churches and cathedrals, evangelical and otherwise, which had enjoyed full congregations in previous years, were, beginning in the early decades of this century, virtually empty. This condition forced the church leadership of England to come to grips with the problem of communication and renewal several years before leaders in this country were required to do so.

Erik Routley had this to say about the religious situation in England in the 1950s:

> The hold of the church on those people whom Moody and Sankey evangelized has for the moment weakened. Entertainment and information are now universal, and the church finds itself a struggling competitor in fields, where for a millenium and a half, it has held the monopoly.[12]

The musical answer to the need for revival was to turn to the idioms of the secular world, as had been done in earlier periods of church history. This latest borrowing from the marketplace seems to have begun with the music of Geoffrey Beaumont in the Church of England with his *Twentieth Century Folk Mass*.[13] Harold Myra and Dean Merrill, pointing out the church's needs as well as Beaumont's "answer" in the mid-fifties, stated:

> Catholics, Episcopalians and other formalists have turned on to folk music. As early as 1956, an East London vicar told composer Geoffrey Beaumont that he was "deeply concerned that nothing had been written since the Elizabethans, which can properly be called a folk mass." He said the music of the Anglican Church was totally foreign to the majority of Englishmen, and so Beaumont responded by writing *Folk Mass* in a pop style.[14]

The phenonemon of utilizing popular idioms in recent years did not start, then, with evangelicals, but with the liberal liturgical groups. In fact, for several years the evangelicals would have no part of it. The revival came from outside fundamentalism, and was essentially a renewal of "language." It followed in the wake of the more recent translations of Scripture, and was simultaneous with the period of new liturgies and of new worship languages and action.

---

12. Routley, *The Church and Music,* p. 204.

13. The appendix contains a selected list of examples of popular musical styles which have been appropriated for use by the church.

14. Myra and Merrill, *Rock, Bach, and Superschlock,* p. 107.

In a recent interview, Donald Hustad evaluated this musical revival:

> It has been a part of the new existentialist mood—significant experience. "Have a significant experience." It has a relationship to Pentecostalism, that in our irrational day we don't expect meaning, . . . just have some sort of a psychic experience. This is what the new music comes out of. We are reacting to human need, to the mood of our day. The music does not present deep theology. It may not be untrue. It just presents some kind of a mood. The movement started outside the church, then moved into the liberal church; then it moved to the evangelical church.
>
> Suddenly all the emotional manipulating of two hundred years of revivalism is accepted by the liberal.[15]

Periods of church renewal do not usually begin with a large group of people from within the church. Renewal may, in fact, come from the rebel in the church. The church by nature is conservative and often implicitly defends the view that the status quo is somehow God-ordered. When the church reaches the point of spiritual stagnation, renewal will normally come from a small number of believers who set revival in motion.

> Sometimes they may even alienate themselves from the church in the process. For example, St. Francis of Assisi, Savanarola, Charles Wesley all broke away for purposes of renewal. Invariably one of the means of renewal is new hymnody. Also, invariably, because the old language is associated with the church, this [old] language is looked upon as being somewhat corrupt because the church is corrupt. The church is dead—the symbols are judged to be dead. We need new forms in order to get new life.[16]

Renewal has always brought changes in form, whether in the Oxford Movement or in any other movement, even the Counter-Reformation. The folk or lay-oriented renewal movements are usually also evangelistic movements; this has been true particularly in the last two centuries.

---

15. Hustad, interview.
16. Hustad, interview.

St. Francis of Assisi was a renewalist, though the Roman Catholic church would never call him an evangelist. Much of the Lutheran movement was political, but it was renewal. St. Francis came on the scene at a low moral ebb in the Roman church. He brought true piety to the church after a startling conversion experience. He became an ascetic, a traveling preacher through Italy; [he] had little bands of followers, preaching and bringing spiritual life to a dead church. ... Luther and Calvin [brought] renewal to the church, [as] the Wesleys brought renewal to the church of their day. Everyone had been baptized; everyone was in the church, but there was no vital Christian living.[17]

The Dilemma of the Evangelical Church

Church music has changed very rapidly and radically in the last twenty years. This is true of nearly all fellowships of the Christian church: evangelical, liberal Protestant, and Catholic. We will limit the rest of this study to the popular-style music in evangelical Protestant churches.

As we have indicated, the modern utilization of pop styles for purposes of witness began *outside* of the evangelical church. Ironically, it is in this church alone that one would normally expect such a practice to start. After all, the evangelical had existed for two hundred years with his heritage of pietist music and a penchant for evangelism. However, in the 1950s, many evangelical musicians were struggling with a schizophrenic conflict which could be called "the tyranny of art" versus "the tyranny of the Holy Spirit."[18] The conservatory-trained musician regards music as art, but in evangelism music is viewed as a tool of communication. To the serious evangelical musician, this conflict has caused much frustration.

To an observant musician outside the evangelical fellowship, it would have seemed as if the evangelical church of the 1950s had a music program of almost calculated mediocrity. When the evangelical musician compared his music with the music of the liberal church across the street, he developed an

17. Ibid.
18. Ibid.

inferiority complex. Evangelical detractors wanted to know why he was singing "waltz music" and "entertainment music" and calling it worship music. Another cause for frustration was the series of writings questioning the quality of church music by such respected musicians as Archibald Davison, Canon Douglas, and Joseph Ashton.

During this time many evangelicals did a great deal of soul-searching. They reaped many benefits as a result, for finer quality became evident. The choir music improved; there were more great hymns of doctrine, more objective hymns of worship and devotion which had been totally ignored for so long. The service music was improved and better organs were installed. Speaking of these evangelical musicians, Donald Hustad said,

> Just about the time we all agreed we should all go uphill, moving upward in all of our church music exposures, both up front and in the pew, suddenly we met the competition—the Lutherans, the Episcopalians, the Catholics—those who had so long beckoned us to come on up to better things. And what was the competition doing? They were coming back *down hill,* singing folk hymns and strumming guitars! What a shock for evangelicals![19]

Experiments with Jazz

Often new musical forms and styles which are at first refused and scorned by the church become serious and sophisticated forms which influence church music. This was true of jazz, to some extent, earlier in the century. (The jazz style has not been extensively used in evangelism, however.)

When legitimate jazz was popular in the 1930s, the attitudes of church leadership were much different from the attitudes of today's leaders. Leaders in the 1930s and 1940s were quite satisfied with the status of their churches and their music, for in those years there was a distinct line of separation between which music was sacred and which was secular. Harold Best has said:

---

19. Hustad, lecture.

When jazz reached its cultural heights in the thirties and forties, evangelicals were so dualistic about the sacred and secular that they wouldn't borrow from the world as overtly as they do now. The associations were too bad and evangelical leaders of today who are in their fifties and sixties don't have the associations with rock that they might have had with jazz. Therefore they still condemn jazz even though they don't condemn rock.[20]

Jazz, to the serious jazz musician, is a disciplined, sophisticated, and evolved art form, one which requires improvisational ability. But this was not always what was meant when the term *jazz* was used to identify a certain sacred style. In many cases, what has been called jazz was not jazz at all, but a simplified, watered down, foot-stomping, stage band, "gospel" style—a far cry from legitimate jazz. The term *jazz* became a catch-all for any music which seemed too popularly secular and therefore inappropriate for use in church.

Many evangelicals of the 1940s and 1950s were fighting the battle to condemn "gospel jazz." It was, as Routley stated, "another illustration of the complexity of the problem of *authority* in music."[21] Routley expressed his amazement that those who complain longest and loudest against light secular influences in church music are those who champion emotional, ecstatic preaching and improvised prayer.[22] All of these adjectives also describe jazz.

It is important to remember that jazz has its roots in the Negro spiritual, a form decidedly sacred in origin. Stephen Hall has expressed the early Negro spiritual/jazz relationship in this way:

The actual association of jazz with religion began when jazz was still an embryo within the spirituals and work songs of negro slaves. These spirituals were the very essence of religious expression for these oppressed people.[23]

---

20. Harold Best, "Music: Offerings of Creativity," p. 13.
21. Routley, *Words, Music and the Church,* p. 74.
22. Ibid., p. 111.
23. Stephen Hall, "The Christian Folk Musical: A Foundational Study," p. 31.

Perhaps the following statements by recognized musicians and church music philosophers will help to clarify one viewpoint.

A leader in the use of jazz in church music, Heinz Werner Zimmermann, says that "jazz is the folk music of the twentieth century. A composer of our time can draw stimulation from it as composers of earlier times could draw stimulation from their national folk music."[24]

Ed Summerlin, known for his *Requiem for Mary Jo* and his work on contemporary religious television programs, has spoken for the cause of jazz idioms in the church. He reveals, "I felt for years that bringing jazz into the church was a kind of end in itself, and that the reflective qualities of jazz improvisation were especially suited for the church."[25] Erik Routley supports this view when he writes:

> Church music is not concert music: it is, or ought to be, much more a music of personal involvement. Jazz is [this] and it can at least invite us to question our ghastly Protestant silence, our "relevance," in our church music.[26]

Incidentally, some studies have been devoted to the blues, the Negro spiritual, jazz, and rock and roll, but very little attention has been given to the source of this music: the black church of America. The interested reader is directed to an excellent study on this subject by Horace Boyer.[27]

Some church music analysts try to compare the modern sacred rock movement with that of jazz in the church in an earlier generation. But those who oppose rock music in the church say the comparison breaks down when one examines the *intentions* of rock music as opposed to those of jazz.

The question which all contemporary musical evangelists must answer is whether or not today's rock idiom is a true, genuine "style of the folk." This is a very complex issue, with strong advocates on both sides. Few of them are very logical

24. Heinz Werner Zimmermann, "And All That Jazz," p. 34.

25. Ed Summerlin, "Maybe We All Missed the Point," p. 23.

26. Erik Routley, *Is Jazz Music Christian?*, pp. 9–10.

27. Horace C. Boyer, "An Analysis of Black Church Music with Examples Drawn from Services in Rochester, New York."

or biblically or historically accurate. Most simply make emotional pleas for their position.

The proponents of gospel rock maintain that this "popularizing" of church music for witness is merely the latest example of what the church has done with its music throughout its history. Many opponents say that rock music is intrinsically evil. In trying to strengthen their case, the opponents cite the most extreme rock music examples and degenerate lifestyles and habits of hard rock musicians.

Sacred rock advocates are among those who insist that there is nothing inherently evil in any musical style. But the opposition counters that this music was inspired by wickedness from the beginning, and therefore nothing good can be found in it or come from it. Unlike rock, jazz had a pure, honest, even sacred beginning as found in the Negro spiritual. Jazz was concerned with the "basic hopes and protests of humanity."[28]

But that is just what today's sacred rock music is concerned with, claim the church musicians who use this idiom. They might be correct. The alternatives are either nonexistent or completely undesirable to them. Their debate with traditional church musicians is still unsettled.

---

28. Routley, *Words, Music and the Church,* p. 113.

PART TWO:

Witness Music Since 1960

Chapter 7

Philosophies, Experiments, and Practices of the 1960s

Upheaval in the Arts

Howard D. McKinney, writing in 1967, noted that the arts "are in the midst of a transitional period that marks the end of one great creative epoch and the beginning of an era of uncertainty, unknown experimentation, a transition that may well take at least a century."[1] McKinney went on to describe some of the issues which emerged in the chaos of the 1960s. Contending that the minister of church music must "positionalize" himself, McKinney stated that he must also distinguish

> ... the past from the future, the conservative from the radical, what may appear to be old-fashioned and dull, ...based on the experience and traditions of the past, from the youthful experimentation and radical action suited to the necessities of today and the hopes for tomorrow.... As a matter of fact, busy as he must be in two spheres of modern creative activity, he will become more and more involved in this growing conflict of ideas and it becomes obvious that his whole future, as well as that of the entire world of church music, will depend upon the way this conflict is resolved.[2]

---

1. Howard D. McKinney, "Winds of Change," p. 2.
2. Ibid.

These statements introduce to our study certain phenomena in church music of the 1960s. The church has been confronted with many forms of music which seem alien to its tradition. There have been supporters of jazz, pop music, aleatoric music, twelve-tone music, and electronic music. The question of the legitimacy of these forms has been followed by much controversy.

Certainly the total scope of church music styles is so large that any style will be foreign to some congregation somewhere. A church musician's reaction to unfamiliar styles will depend on his musical and social background, the location of his ministry, the people to whom he ministers, and the age in which he is living.

Writing about new attempts in church music, James Vail says:

> Much of the musical, liturgical and multimedia experimentation that has been going on is healthy. The traditional overconservatism of the church in the arts is at last being challenged and in not a few cases the church has been involved in some artistic pioneering.[3]

There are those who maintain that the 1960s began a "new romanticism."[4] Romanticism normally implies a popular artistic outburst. The great increase in musical creativity seems to be consistent evidence of a new romantic period.

The Outreach of the Non-Evangelical Fellowships

In 1903 the Roman church made one of the strongest, seemingly final attempts to control the music in its churches. In that year the *Motu Proprio* warned its members against the use of inappropriate music for the church service. Sixty years later, in 1963, the Roman church again made a plea to its constituency, but this time the plea was of a different sort.

---

3. James R. Vail, "Values in Church Music: A Reassessment," p. 10.

4. Dr. Charles C. Hirt has stated this view in various classes at the University of Southern California as well as in national conventions such as the American Choral Directors Association Convention in Seattle, Washington in 1968.

By an overwhelming vote, the Roman Catholic hierarchy of Vatican II decided to permit the use of vernacular instead of Latin in certain parts of the Mass, and to encourage the singing participation of the people.

This was part of the evidence that the church needed a new "language." In succeeding years, the market was flooded with Scripture translations, new vernacular liturgies, and more of the "people's music." As we noted earlier, the evangelical musician had been

> "upstaged" in his familiar role of music evangelist by the competition, by the liturgical, more liberal fellowships who were the first to use some of the new forms and idioms, and they were beating the evangelicals at their own game,[5]

using the music of the secular world for attraction to the church. And it was working for them just as it had worked for the evangelical church in former years. Now, suddenly, the evangelical could alter his pattern and premise of musical condescension which had characterized his music for so long.

Experiments with Sacred "Pop" Music

Following the advent of the Beatles in the early sixties, gospel folk and gospel rock music appeared in England. Traditional evangelical groups were horrified, claiming that this worldly music was not fit to carry a holy message. Nevertheless, some of this music was carried on by ministers of the Church of England who were seeking contact with unevangelized people. Other musical groups were under the auspices of more evangelically-oriented organizations. Regardless of sponsorship, however, the new musical evangelism was seldom the work of professional musicians, or even of those in the world of "pop" or professional entertainment.

This was one of the results of the revolution toward sacred pop music in the 1960s: an increased participation by the amateur musician. A greater number of would-be musicians and composers now felt that they were able to create an

---

5. Hustad, lecture.

effective form of musical communication. For church music this urge to create had both advantages and liabilities. It encouraged more people to make attempts at creativity, and in some cases, new talent was discovered. There was even a receptive audience for the music of the less talented writers. Certainly a good amount of witness music was produced for specific congregations, audiences, or settings to be used for that moment alone, and not to be commercialized and permanent.

But, as Erik Routley says:

> The consequence is that it comes out as well-intentioned but imitative; and the model imitated is sometimes ecclesiastical rather than secular, so that, in such tunes ... we get in effect the imitation of an old ecclesiastical imitation of historic music hall.[6]

The Salvation Army

One of the traditional evangelical organizations which had an effective musical outreach at the start of the sacred pop phenomenon in England was the Salvation Army. In Britain as in America, this group has maintained an important and distinctive musical ministry with its street-corner musical groups which play, sing, and preach. Their music has been an example of an effort to reach people with a distinctive cultural language. The argument of its founder, William Booth, was that the Church of England was not reaching the common working man. But Booth did so by using the working man's music. This initial purpose has been carried out in those urban areas where sufficient musical talent has been available.

Originally, the music of the Salvation Army was functional music at best—a brass band to attract people on the street corner, followed by march music to "march the crowd" into the chapel. And, even though the music of the Salvation Army has not been a part of mainstream evangelism, through popular sacred music (at least of the more recent commercial type) it has had an important influence in local settings.

---

6. Routley, *Twentieth Century Church Music*, p. 172.

The best example of the trend is provided by the "Joy-strings," a group of five attractive youths in Salvation Army uniforms, who offer their own versions of modern gospel music in British night clubs, "pubs," and church-sponsored coffee bars. They also appear in cathedrals and more conventional settings.[7]

The Joystrings were organized in 1963 for the express purpose of evangelism. However, because their performance was typical of most rock groups, the words were difficult to understand due to the loud guitars, organ, and drums. The effectiveness of any evangelistic communication must be questioned when the message is overpowered by the medium.

In many of these performances it appeared that the audience was more interested in the beat or the style of the rock music than in the words of the songs. Hustad points out that even when groups like the Joystrings alternate between secular and sacred songs, with careful planning, a well-placed song of witness or testimony can be very effective when used as a counter to a purely secular number. Many groups, both in Europe and the United States are totally committed and sincere in their work, believing that theirs is a special calling to share the gospel with people who might otherwise not listen.

From England to America

A British church musician, Cecil Allen, described the pop styles of the 1960s as used by the churches in his country.

No doubt the aim is to be "with it," so far as modern young people are concerned, and thus to draw no line of distinction between the type of music in which they are soaked and that which we use in our approach to God. As distinct from the Sankey type of tune, these "beat" tunes are far from simple in their composition, and do not fall easily within the range of the less competent performers. Also, to emphasize their resemblance to what young people are accustomed to hear from "pop" singers and "top ten" dance bands, most of the tunes are provided with continuo bars between verse and verse, so

---

7. Donald Hustad, "Entertainment in Evangelism," p. 2.

that there is no pause in the continuity of the music from the start to the finish of the hymn.[8]

There are several ironies associated with the recent sacred pop music phenomenon. One is that the recent revolution in musical evangelism began in an unexpected sector of Christianity—the liberal, liturgical fellowships of England— in the early 1960s and was quickly conveyed to America. Many conservative American ministers, musicians, and laymen hoped that the sacred jazz, folk, or rock experiments of the sixties would be isolated phenomena of minor consequence. There were evangelical American church music composers in the fifties and sixties who were on the cutting edge of acceptable evangelical musical style. Most of these, however, exerted only a small influence on the overall idiom of musical witness.

Another irony with regard to this new music for witness is that during the sixties this music was not directly associated with organized mass evangelism. The larger evangelistic organizations tended to stay clear of the more extreme styles of sacred pop. The more progressive styles were utilized by those groups that engaged strictly in musical evangelism. In their music there were many styles within styles, proliferating from hard rock, folk, gospel, country, and music designed for Jewish outreach (such as that sung by the group called "The Liberated Wailing Wall").

Many people feel that in the later sixties and in the seventies the church was in the pattern of renewal, which includes evangelism. Generally, evangelism is preceded by renewal— the church is renewed from within, then it evangelizes. As a matter of fact, it might be difficult to use the term "evangelism" in conjunction with the recent sacred pop music phenomena, since most of the musicians that produce this type of music are not associated with evangelists. Many of them would claim that they are "on their own," that the music itself is the evangelism.[9]

---

8. Allen, *Hymns and the Christian Faith,* p. 112.

9. A more thorough discussion of the distinctions between music which is specifically for evangelism and music which is more generally for outreach and witness will be encountered in chap. 10.

Musical Evangelism "On Tour"

Most of the progressive musical evangelism today is being done by itinerant music groups, rather than by independent individual musicians. In this generation a number of popular traveling evangelistic organizations have appeared. In naming a few of these, it is most logical to start with the Spurrlows, a musical team organized by Thurlow Spurr. This organization was molded and disciplined into one of the slickest Christian entertainment groups of this country. For several years the Spurrlows traveled under the auspices of the Chrysler Motor Corporation. The Spurrlows served as an example to other later, similar groups which include "The New Folk" of Campus Crusade for Christ; "The Continentals" which now have several traveling teams; the Oral Roberts University "World Action Singers," which have been on national television since 1969; and several Youth for Christ music groups which have traveled in the United States and overseas since 1961 ("Soul Concern," "Random Sample," "The New World Singers").

Groups which have had a very effective outreach in the 1970s are Derric Johnson's "Regeneration"; "Free Spirit," a group under the auspices of the Free Methodist Church; "The Sound Alliance" of the Christian and Missionary Alliance fellowship; Roger Breland's "Truth"; "The Second Chapter of Acts"; and "The Liberated Wailing Wall" of the Jews-for-Jesus organization. "The Life Action Singers," a group started in the early 1970s by evangelist Del Fehsenfeld, perform sacred concerts with emphasis on revival and evangelism. Their chief ministry consists of week-long meetings in which, in addition to their musical performances, the singers engage in counseling. Their music is viewed as supportive of the main goal of revival and evangelism.

Most organizations like these consist of capable musicians under qualified leadership. The problem facing many church music leaders now, however, is what to do with the hundreds of groups which have sprung up, many of which have far less talent. Although it is dangerous to make spiritual judgments, it has seemed that some groups pretend to be evangelistic simply because they are not able to succeed in the world of secular entertainment. A British writer on the sacred pop music scene in England talks of the "growing band of musicians and singers on the road for Jesus, at least supposedly."[10]

Gospel music is a big business, and quite often the audience is less demanding as far as excellence is concerned. One wonders if, for some of these groups, gospel music is only a steppingstone to something more lucrative and more openly secular. On the other hand, it should be pointed out that the reverse is also true. There have been successful secular entertainers who, because of their conversion to Christianity and a disillusionment with their work, have left secular entertainment for the cause of Christian witness.

This type of musical witness is a part of the continuing effort of organizations such as the Salvation Army and itinerant groups to take the gospel where the people are. A problem sometimes arises, however, when groups like the Joystrings become so popular. Their kind of music generally has a very quick appeal to young people, who soon view the traditional music of the church as comparatively unexciting. The unfortunate result of this shift in taste is a tendency to discard the other styles.

It is important that the church provide its young people with vital, interesting musical opportunities. If this is not done, youth will create or find its own styles and opportunities. British church leaders could have given their young people an appealing style based on the fine heritage of English folk song. When this was not done, young people turned to untrained and undisciplined musical idioms.

It is estimated that there were probably more than two thousand religious "beat groups" in England in the mid-1960s, many of which were sincere in their efforts at musical evangelism. An organization known as the "Musical Gospel Outreach" trained groups for this kind of work.

We have seen that the sacred rock phenomenon now current in the United States had many of its roots in Britain, though the deeper roots (i.e., spirituals and jazz), were certainly American as far as the overall movement is concerned. How much of this style for sacred music actually was taken

---

10. Tony Jasper, *Jesus in a Pop Culture,* p. 107.

from Britain is uncertain. It is probable that the church musicians in this country looking for something new, exciting, and attractive would eventually have usurped the rock style anyway. Which country led which into this new stylistic medium is not very important now. The point is that the church in America did embrace many of the marketplace styles to attract those outside the fold of Christianity.

One can remember quite clearly some of the first highly advertised attempts by liberal churches in the late 1950s and early 1960s to attract people from the community by using jazz settings of the Mass. National leaders in the liberal movement had diagnosed their average local church as "very sick." This sickness also involved their music, for their large pipe organs, complex anthems and cantatas, and professional musical leadership were not doing the job.

Sacred Folk Music Experiments

The music of the church in any age, including music of witness and evangelism, must fit the needs and serve the people of that age. If churches wish to serve the religious needs of the common folk, they cannot afford to neglect the best of the folk music and folk spirituals even though this music may never qualify as classic.

Indeed, there has been a resurgence of interest in folk singing in the United States, and church music has not been unaffected by it. In its purest and simplest form a folk song is sung by a soloist or very small vocal group, usually accompanied by a guitar. The older, traditional folk songs were generally rustic, rural work songs. More recently, however, the folk song has often been a song of protest, anger, or rebellion. Some of this is especially difficult for the church to accept because much of the protest is against the organized church itself, which has been to some protesters just another establishment organization. Routley says:

> The fact that atheist anarchism and communism are prominent among the folk singers makes the church understandably cautious about their techniques. Moreover, folk singing is

rapidly becoming a commercial cult like pop, and its under-
ground culture does share some of the less lovely attributes of
the jazz culture.[11]

It should be clear that folk music—true folk music, that
is—should be perfectly acceptable for gifted Christian musicians to use for evangelistic purposes. Two significant distinctions of the folk song are that the words are very important,
and that the folk song represents the general mood of the
culture. These songs can be used to express the world's need,
and, when sung by a soloist or folk-singing group, can communicate ideas that many hymns do not. Donald Hustad asks:

> Why not use the folk song medium to present gospel truth?
> At any rate, we join the plea for realistic songs of salvation, in
> which we temper the ecstatic declaration "And now I am
> happy all the day" with the honest admission that Christian
> faith doesn't eliminate all your problems but does help you
> know where to find their resolution.[12]

Traditionally, of course, sacred folk songs have not been
associated with matters of dogma. Rather they have served as
devotional songs for the home, as Christmas or children's
songs. During the nineteenth century they were used a great
deal in missionary societies and religious circles in general. In
a few cases they have found their way into hymnals, at least
into the appendices.

Before the church musician can determine his philosophy
and position on the use of folk music, he must formulate an
acceptable definition of sacred folk music. Just what is a true
sacred music expression of the folk? In the last two decades,
this question has not been satisfactorily settled. Some would
maintain that all of today's popular styles (rock music in its
many forms, ballads, country and western music) should be
regarded as folk styles since they are such a dominant force in
society. Some may regard all of these popular idioms as folk
music, but they are not in the same category as most true folk
music of earlier ages. As James Vail states:

---

11. Routley, *Words, Music and the Church*, p. 124.
12. Donald Hustad, "Shall We Demythologize Our Hymns?" p. 9.

The "folk music" is not folk music at all but is simply commercially composed music "for the folk." The frequent appeal to historical precedent to justify the borrowing of "music from the marketplace" for use in the church provides an argument of questionable strength. In the first place the secular and folk music employed for church use by Martin Luther, the renaissance composers, Bach, Vaughan Williams and many others at certain times in the past was of far more durable stuff, and parallels today's expendable commercial pop music very little.[13]

Sacred folk-style music has proved, however, to be a positive influence in Christian witness. Much of it is very good, solid, and appropriate as a church music idiom. In seeking to promote lasting values in church music, of course, modern folk music alone is inadequate. But folk music may be as close as we can come to music which spontaneously expresses the faith of the majority of the people. One folk-singing couple says:

> Folk songs are songs that everyone can sing, anywhere, anytime. They can be used as personal devotion; they can be sung when you can't find the words to pray. Folk songs bring the music of the church back to the people. They are, perhaps, the form best suited for the renewal of our faith and witness.[14]

The Youth Musical

The youth folk-musical phenomenon was born in the late 1960s. The Southern Baptists had their "Good News," a musical by Bob Oldenburg which borrowed more from earlier idioms than from the contemporary idioms.[15]

In 1968 Ralph Carmichael and Kurt Kaiser jointly created "Tell It Like It Is." In 1969 they wrote "Natural High," with even the title reflecting the drug culture so prevalent at the

13. Vail, "Values in Church Music," p. 10.

14. Barbara Hillard and A. J. Hillard, "Folk Music: Fresh Wind or Storm?" p. 8.

15. For further information and critical analysis of this musical, see the thesis by Stephen F. Hall, "The Christian Folk Musical: A Foundational Study."

time. These earliest attempts at folk musical writing were not particularly bold in the use of Christian doctrine, but young people in America were more than ready to accept the new sound. However, the parallels of this music (and sometimes the lyrics) to the music of the drug scene were shocking to the conservative Christian.

"For Heaven's Sake" (1961), according to Phillip Land-grave, has one of the most advanced texts in all of folk music literature.[16] However, it was too deeply theological for most churches and the music was outdated. Most of these early musicals borrowed from musical idioms that were popular five, ten, or even twenty years earlier. Only with the advent of such musicals as "Tell It Like It Is" and "Celebrate Life" did Christian composers begin to use the light folk styles of their day, though even in these there were "throwbacks." Nearly all folk musicals are eclectic in style, rather than classical and unified in style. One problem with the folk musical is that it is a dated, rather than timeless, piece of music. By the time the church begins to use it, it is already out of style. As Landgrave said,

> The popular styles are always accessible, but they are always at the edge, at the hind edge, of accessibility. They get on the "caboose" of the popular trends.[17]

Other musicals followed: "Life" and "Love" by Otis Skillings; "Show Me" by Jimmie and Carol Owens; and "New Vibrations" and "Requiem for a Nobody" by Tedd Smith (pianist for the Billy Graham Crusade team).[18]

Pop Music

Sacred pop music is as hard to define as sacred folk music. Pop music can be seen as contemporary music which appeals to the masses, generally of urban communities. Pop tunes are

---

16. Phillip Landgrave, interview held at Southern Baptist Theological Seminary, Louisville, Kentucky, April 15, 1977.

17. Ibid.

18. A more complete list of folk-style musicals appears in the appendix.

not only difficult to define, they are also difficult to categorize because of the many hybrid varieties which exist today. It is not at all uncommon to hear a combination of baroque or classical styles mingling with strains of rock, country and western, jazz, or blues. In contrast to some of the pop and rock music of the 1960s and early 1970s, these musical styles are increasingly produced by serious, well-trained musicians.

Generally, however, pop tunes are very simple, sometimes showing an amazing similarity to gospel hymn tunes (this accounts for some of the cross-appearances in hymnbooks and the "hit" charts in recent years). Many pop tunes are so poor that they would not be welcomed for any purpose by church musicians, but other tunes and styles are good and have been borrowed by various church groups for informal use. "O Happy Day" and "Amazing Grace" are songs which have been found in both church and marketplace music. Ralph Carmichael's composition, "Love Is Surrender" is available with two sets of lyrics in an attempt to make it acceptable to either church congregations or secular audiences.

Although copyright restrictions prohibit wholesale use of pop tunes, the influence of these styles has been felt in evangelistic music for many years. There is little reason why the Christian musician in his search for an evangelistic musical expression should not be able to use those influences which are musically worthy and honest.

However, much of secular pop music is involved with vast commercial publicity, the youthful homage of pop singers, and creating a great amount of noise. Some aspects of recent evangelistic techniques parallel several of these elements, as Routley explains,

> ... in saturation publicity, in the mystique surrounding a glamorous preacher, and in the producing, not precisely of an enormous and oppressive noise, but of an impression of overwhelming power and competence through the big, uniformed, regimented choir.... I merely point out that the evangelistic techniques of some contemporary crusaders are pop techniques: essentially undistinguished music is "pro-

duced" with bands, electronic organs, large choirs and solo-ists, so as to sound impressive.[19]

Some pop-style evangelistic music normally considered to be dull is often made more palatable by a smooth performance or special arrangement. The marvels of twentieth-century electronics have helped many sacred music performers, both in recordings and live. Many mediocre songs, both old and new, have been reset and rearranged, then given to a singer who can be aided by such devices as echo (in live or recorded renditions), or overdubbing in the recording studio.

Attempts at "Sacred Rock"

The average evangelical church musician usually has noth-ing to do with any of the avant-garde musical forms, choosing rather the more traditional music of his heritage or the mod-erate popular styles. These idioms of pop and folk do not generally create a serious problem in today's evangelical church. Rather, the heated debate in evangelical music circles in recent years has to do with the use of rock styles.

It should be stated early in this discussion that proportion-ately very little of the extreme forms of rock music is used in churches. Still, the influences can be seen in much of recent music of the evangelical. The use of the rock idiom in its varied styles is probably the most emotionally debated, least comprehended problem of evangelical church music in the last ten years.

Most writers either condemn rock in all of its forms as a satanic diversion, or they commend it without qualification. One of the best books on the subject is *Rock Music* by William J. Schafer. Schafer points out how wide and varied are the opinions on rock music in general:

> Opinion has ranged down a long continuum from hysterical condemnation to hysterical adulation, with every shade and mixture between. Some Christian groups have condemned rock as only a demonic source of corruption, an external man-ifestation of a "drug culture" which is totally depraved. The

19. Routley, *Words, Music and the Church*, p. 118.

other end of the spectrum is the radical utopian assertion that rock is the most profound source of liberation, self-insight, and cosmic knowledge. A middle ground might be that rock is often a positive source of joy, of physical release and healthy exuberance; it may also be a symptom of deep social and personal disturbances and problems, leading sometimes to excesses of mind and body.[20]

One cannot ignore the fact that rock music has had a very close connection with some of the worst forms of carnality and corruption. Most Christians are uncomfortable with a cult or idiom which has been associated with drugs and sexual freedom. It is interesting to note, however, that most Christians are usually not troubled with the music of Wagner despite his personal lifestyle, nor are they particularly distressed about Beethoven's music regardless of his sometimes questionable ethics.

Recently, for many progressive evangelical church musicians interested in the latest mode of communication for purposes of outreach, the answer seemed to be a certain kind of sacred rock music. This brand of sacred rock was neither reformed nor transformed, but merely watered down and "institutionalized"—with just enough imitation of secular rock to give a feeling of excitement and "relevance." The problem is that if a church musician uses one type of musical expression with a week-by-week consistency, he is bound to alienate some. A straight rock or pop diet will offend the person with a developed taste for fine music, driving him with his artistic sensitivity back to the world to find a higher level of expression. He may assume that artistic authenticity simply does not exist in the church. He may also conclude that Christianity attempts to blend spirituality with artistic and cultural sterility.

One author claims that the blues are comparable to the early Christian chant, for they fulfill a similar purpose—to provide the singer with emotional release.[21] Before condemning such a comparison it must be noted that many

---

20. William J. Schafer, *Rock Music: Where It's Been, What It Means, Where It's Going,* p. 80.

21. J. Wood, "Reflections on the Nature of Jazz," p. 120.

church music historians and Bible and language scholars regard the "spiritual songs" (Col. 3:16; Eph. 5:19) of the New Testament to be improvised, ecstatic utterances, as opposed to the more learned, memorized, predictable Psalms and hymns.

Some have compared the church's objections to today's rock with the conservative reaction to jazz in the previous generation. But the more progressive musical evangelists were perhaps too eager for a new language of communication—they did not wait until rock music attained any degree of artistic respectability.

Actually, neither jazz nor rock in its most extreme forms ever became a dominant force in musical outreach. A comparison of rock and jazz, particularly in their rhythmic construction, would show rock to give more emphasis to the strong, principal beats. Rock's steady rhythmic beat is often more solid than jazz, which tends to accentuate the syncopated beat.

Rock Musicals

With church attendance declining, church leaders and musicians looked more and more to the popular idioms to attract people. Most of these styles and influences led eventually to the staged sacred musical. The two main initial examples of this were "Jesus Christ, Superstar" and "Godspell." The great debate continued.

In discussing the musical, "Jesus Christ, Superstar," Alan Rich writes:

> A lively fight has developed among church leaders of all faiths as to whether such an entertainment does or does not constitute a blasphemy, and Jewish spokesmen have objected to the fact that the words of the show seem to indicate that the Jews in ancient Jerusalem were clearly guilty for the death of Christ. Further arguments rage among those who find it pure trash.
>
> ... Naturally a work like "Superstar" is going to shock people, since it suddenly brings religious music up to date with a huge forward leap. It fills the vacuum that the conservatism of the church itself has helped to create.[22]

---

22. Rich, "Religion with a Rock Beat," p. 17, 19.

The strong negative reaction to "Superstar" and "Godspell" on the part of some musicians may be fully justified. However, the proponents of rock musicals can give valid evidence of the importance of church dramas and church mysteries of earlier centuries. In citing the historical evidence of religion on the stage, Ernestine Guglielmo writes:

> Musical versions of Christ's life have been done for centuries in passions, oratorios and masses by symphonic giants like Bach and Handel and Stravinsky, but seldom has the story of Christ been brought to the secular stage in such human form. The difference is that Jesus Christ comes alive as a man in contemporary terms through the popular musical idiom.[23]

It does not appear that the rock musicals like "Superstar" and "Godspell" were particularly important in the ministry of evangelicals. But even if these musicals seldom found their way into churches, their influence was felt. Several writers in nationally syndicated music columns predicted just how influential the sacred rock musical would be. One of these said,

> The rock thumpings always have carried a hint of gospel beat, but now it's coming on loud and strong, breaking out in the lyrics. It's usually not in traditionally pious terminology, and some of it may not make much theological sense, but it nevertheless registers a religious inclination.
>
> A trade magazine, *Entertainment World,* predicts the religious themes are likely to become more prominent. Noting that "rock 'n' roll has solid foundation in gospel music" in rudimentary origins, the magazine adds: "Since this is a period when rock musicians are exploring their musical roots, it is not surprising that religion is finding its way into their music."[24]

The Jesus Movement

The Jesus Movement has been of considerable influence in gospel rock. Musicians of this movement have made regular

23. *Scranton Times* (Pa.), December 31, 1971.

24. George Cornell, "Modern Music Featuring More Gospel Sounds," *Scranton Times* (Pa.), April 29, 1970, p. 48.

appearances with programs of sacred rock music and personal testimony. Many of these groups have produced record albums which are available in both secular and religious outlets and are heard on certain Christian and secular radio stations. In fact, the ministry of evangelism through gospel recordings has been extremely effective in recent years. Since very little contemporary secular music says anything substantive, sacred recording helps fill that vacuum by joining the resurgence of popular evangelical expression. According to James Pennington,

> Christian music now has an opportunity that it has not had before. Christians have the message that can change lives, but to reach today's young people it must be presented in a way that will catch their attention.
> ... The best way to present the Gospel of Christ ... is to use the right bait. The bait ... is contemporary music.[25]

The rock music of the Jesus Movement appears to be much freer, more personal, and more intimate than other types of sacred rock.

> The main differences in Jesus music are in the lyrics (it's street language) and in the fact that nobody here is afraid of a straight rock sound. Not all of it is solid rock, of course, but some is. The whole scene is considerably more natural and unpretentious than what came earlier, probably because Jesus groups don't think as much about church deacons looking over their shoulders.
> In massive festivals all over the country, young people are introduced to Jesus Christ through their straightforward music.
> What it all adds up to is that for the first time since Ira Sankey, we've got a big batch of music that non-Christians can identify with.[26]

Andrae Crouch and the Disciples, Larry Norman, Randy Matthews, The Armageddon Experience, Love Song, Agape, Sound Foundation, and Danny Lee and the Children of Truth head the list as some of the most popular Jesus musicians.

---

25. James M. Pennington, "Rock Music—Love ad infinitum, ad absurdum," p. 21.

26. Myra and Merrill, *Rock, Bach, and Superschlock*, p. 111.

Rock Influence

Has rock music influenced church music today in a broad sense? Because of the difficulty in providing an objective definition of rock music, it is also difficult to pinpoint its influences.[27] Certainly some of the rhythmic figurations have been usurped. There is a new rhythmic honesty and naturalness in much of the new "soft rock" style. It is no longer so stilted. It has a rhythm much closer to the rhythm of everyday speech. When some of this new rhythm was put in print, it was sometimes difficult for the average singer to sightread. After some exposure to it, however, reading became much easier. It became a matter not so much of reading it as simply "feeling it."

Does rock music offer potential for use in church music? According to Philip Landgrave,

> Rock has done with the popular scene ... what jazz did with the popular scene a decade earlier. The first forms of rock were somewhat elementary, even primitive.... Rock was even, in its early stages, less sophisticated than its ... counterpart in the 20s and 30s. But it has now developed and taken off on various tributaries away from the main source. But, under the development of various groups like "Chicago" and a few others, the rock sound has become more and more sophisticated.
>
> Rock in its most sophisticated forms offers musical development. In the popular style at its best some of it is as creative in the improvisatory sense as what was going on in the Baroque period.
>
> It's a chord-figured melody now rather than a figured bass, but the same principle breaks through with individual creativity from certain given material.
>
> In written forms, too, I think rock offers us a musical creativity and some integrity, too.[28]

Hard sacred rock, however, at least in published form, has never been fully accepted by most church music publishers. There were attempts, but hard rock usually requires a certain amount of textual obliteration. The volume of sound needed

---

27. One of the finest series of articles on rock can be found in the *Music Educator's Journal*, November 1969, pp. 43–74.

28. Landgrave, interview.

for hard or acid rock is that of a "mind-blowing" experience. There is little chance of communicating anything other than the total inundation of sound to the point of psychic escape from reality.[29] The responsibility of the church is not to provide escape from reality, but to give answers to contemporary problems through legitimate, biblical means. The lighter, softer rock styles still allow for the communication of the text.

Just how rock music styles will influence church music in the future, whether for purposes of witness or even in the worship service, cannot be determined. History makes it clear that the music of the church will usually reflect the art, culture, and taste of the time. Indeed, if the church does not reflect some of the current culture, it is probably an indication that the church is in need of revival or renewal. As Paul Wohlgemuth predicted:

> Rock music, even though it has had a questionable origin and practice, will in time become a part of the mainstream of church music. Yes, it will be reshaped, it will be refined, it will be adapted; but it will be used. In fact, the 1970s will see a marked acceptance of rock-influenced music in all levels of church music. The rock style will become more familiar to all people, its rhythmic excesses will become refined, and its earlier secular associations will be less remembered.[30]

Experiments with Small Groups

In the late 1960s and early 1970s there appeared what could be regarded as the church's answer to the secular rock music group: the small, informal (frequently church-sponsored) youth singing group. These sprang up all over the country. Some were very good, well-disciplined; others were very bad, with all shades of ability in between. Some groups were strictly local in their outreach, being confined to a neighborhood, Sunday evening evangelistic service, or coffee-house ministry. Others answered the "call of the road" and took to the highways to share their faith through music.

---

29. There have been a few composers who have moved toward the edge of musical acceptability who have since become established—Rick Powell, Tedd Smith, and Ed Summerlin.

30. Paul W. Wohlgemuth, *Rethinking Church Music,* p. 79.

In any case, this was a response (sometimes a healthy one) to the rather sudden realization that young people "finally had something exciting to sing."

In comparing the music of the professional evangelistic groups with the smaller, more intimate, localized church groups, one writer stated,

> There is a difference in the contents of the music, however. The commercial folk rock gospel musicals are openly propagandistic. Their sole aim is mass evangelism. But most of the individual folk artists and the small groups have a very straightforward, almost gutsy honesty to their music. They reveal themselves, their doubts and disappointments as well as their spiritual highs. They may even share their heresies (their music is unscreened), but their simple directness is engaging and refreshing. They refuse to camouflage their lyrics by any false pietism or unexperienced spiritual plateaus.[31]

Although many church musicians have felt that the most important church music ministry is the choir, a large choir can sometimes be impersonal and therefore less effective for evangelism. Since many ministers of music were having difficulty filling their choir lofts, this was an obvious opportunity to develop a more personal, chamber-sized, gospel-singing group.

The Coffee House

A unique specialized ministry designed to confront young people in a smaller, intimate setting is the coffee house. This method of outreach has been successfully used by churches and by large, nondenominational organizations. The Billy Graham Association has experimented with this technique during some of their city-wide crusades. John Pollock describes the coffee house scene during the 1969 New York Crusade:

> Christian pop groups, including the Australian Kinsfolk and the Chicago Extursionists [*sic*] led by an able young musi-

---

31. William J. Peterson, "O, What a Fantastic New Day for Christian Music," p. 17.

cian who had been converted to Christ in 1967 from drugs and "digging the sex scene," played and sang rock and folk music and gave their testimonies, while young people sat ten to a table sipping soft drinks and coffee. Each table had its own counselor who in the intervals between music, would "stimulate dialogue and debate toward Christian commitment."

The idea is to reach them in their medium of music and their idiom of conversation.[32]

Interest in the coffee house for purposes of outreach has waned in the past few years, although some organizations still maintain an active ministry.

Religious Films

Several religious films using sound tracks with sacred folk or rock music have been successful in evangelism. Showing religious films in church was not a new idea in the mid-1960s, but in 1965 when the Billy Graham film, "The Restless Ones," was released, it was one of the first religious films produced to be shown in theaters. In that film, Ralph Carmichael's song, "He's Everything to Me" was introduced, and it subsequently became very popular among young evangelicals for a number of years. In 1966, another Graham film, "For Pete's Sake," was released, again using the music of Carmichael. It contained a song called "The Man," about Christ, who Himself lived on this earth in opposition to the "status quo."

When Carmichael spoke at the mid-winter convention of Youth for Christ International in San Diego, December 1967, he described how he had contemplated the type of music to create for the film, "The Restless Ones."

Two or three years ago I got a call over to World-Wide Pictures and I saw a film there called *The Restless Ones*. ... Whew! I never had anything hit me so hard. I sat there and I watched it. It was without music. I thought "Boy, that really got to me." And then I thought, "How in the world is Billy [Graham] going to get away with that?" You know it was

32. John Pollock, *Crusades*, p. 302.

a real live thing with all the problems I was facing as a dad and problems down to the nitty-gritty where our kids really live and it wasn't like make-believe. It wasn't making nice people nicer and white a lighter shade of white. It was like real people that needed God. . . . I didn't think that people would accept it. So when we got around to thinking about music, it was just unbelievable. The London Philharmonic Strings just didn't make it—or the sweeping glissandos of the harp. It was not that kind of thing. I thought, "Well, then we'd better find out where it is." . . . Anyway, to bring you up to date . . . it [the music in the film] was effective. That's the only reason it was done. I think that's the reason that Billy had nerve enough to spend that kind of money on a film that honest and that gut-real in the first place. We had never done—I had never done—anything like that before for a religious film, let alone for a Graham film. To date, four million people have seen *The Restless Ones* and I can't remember the number of decisions, but it's astronomical. . . . It did work. It did pay off. We, subsequently, have tried to do something like this for the kids on a record, a thing called *For Pete's Sake*. . . . This kind of thing is starting to get to the kids. It's something that their ear is tuned into. I don't have to admit that I like it. I will tell you that I don't particularly care for this kind of music to-day. . . . But anyway, the important thing is that it is done, we're experimenting, and something has to happen to get to the kids. We have to communicate with them.[33]

In a list of composers and arrangers influential in the field of sacred pop, Ralph Carmichael would probably be first. I believe his quotation is significant, not only because it comes from one who has influenced many other sacred-pop writers, but also because his comments were made when the issue of sacred pop was becoming heated.

Use of "New" Instruments

Carmichael's music of this period, as well as the music of most other sacred pop writers in the mid and late sixties, made extensive use of the guitar. A great deal of controversy developed in the church over its use. Many conservative Christians associated this instrument with secular rock music.

---

33. Robert Horner, "The Function of Music in the Youth for Christ Program," pp. 220–21.

In general, the arguments raised against the guitar's use were illogical, extra-biblical, and were often merely emotional.

The harps of the Old and New Testaments are closely related to the Greek *cithara* of the time and were much more like the modern guitar than the harp used in an orchestra There is certainly nothing intrinsically sinful about guitars (or any other instrument, for that matter). No instrument is evil or irreligious simply because secular musicians may have abused it. The Christian musician can assure his people that all instruments will be appropriately used. The Christian listener must give up his prejudices, judging music and instruments objectively on their ability to fill the church's need.

Music in Recent Evangelistic Crusades

The new styles have *not* been overtly associated with organized mass evangelism, for the biggest evangelistic movements have also been the most conservative. Rather, the independent solo singer has been pioneering the pop style, with some of the small vocal groups running a close second.

The music of the Billy Graham crusades has, in fact, been quite conservative. In a study of music of the crusades through 1970,[34] George Stansbury points out that the music has not been as significant as that of earlier mass crusades. He maintains that the musical philosophy and practices of the crusade leaders are closely related to those of the Moody-Sankey revivals. Indeed, many of the evangelistic methods used by earlier historic figures are perpetuated in the Graham meetings. Stansbury writes:

> To limit current crusade musical expressions within narrow stylistic bounds of other generations does little to foster creative musical evangelism. Such limitations have not been characteristic of great evangelistic periods.
> ... By 1970, folk and folk-rock styles had become the norm for all segments of the church. Yet the crusades virtually ignored it. It is paradoxical that instead of creating a revolution as did Sankey, Graham and Barrows [Cliff Bar-

---

34. Stansbury, "Music of the Billy Graham Crusades."

rows, Graham's music director] have ignored a revolution which is all around them.[35]

Stansbury's reasons for arriving at his decision are: (1) The song service has been abbreviated in comparison to former revival crusades; (2) no new hymn material has been taught; and (3) the musical practices and repertoire of the crusades have not influenced or altered American church music to any noticeable extent.

In general it would seem that some of these criticisms apply to Graham's music since 1970. Tedd Smith, the regular crusade pianist, has written some rather progressive witness music in the form of musicals ("New Vibrations," "Requiem for a Nobody"), but this music has not been used, to my knowledge, on any of the crusade platforms. Some guest musicians who have evidenced a more progressive style have been used in certain crusades. Andrae Crouch, for example, has made appearances, but always without his supporting group, the Disciples. He accompanies himself at the piano and does not have the benefit of the extra rhythm and beat which his group provides. From all evidence, therefore, it would appear that the music of the Billy Graham crusades remains conservative and traditional.

---

35. Ibid., p. 317, 321.

Chapter 8

"Pure Pop for Now People"

The "Great Debate" of the 1960s and 1970s

The Pros and Cons of "New Music" for Outreach

In church music history there have been many periods of conflict over the use of current popular styles. Just how heated those debates became is not always clear, though it is probable that opinions on this issue were as strong in the past as they are today. It is unlikely, however, that in any previous time the question of popular music in the church was as problematic or divisive as it has been since the mid-sixties.

Philosophical and practical standpoints range from orthodox conservative church music tradition to unlimited permissiveness. Many feel that music which is to approach God or lead men to Him should have its own distinctive idiom. Others maintain that the church would be far better off if the musical differences between the church and the secular world could be minimized.

The church is conservative in nature (church history validates this) and of all church persuasions, the evangelical is probably the most conservative. Preston Rockholt explains:

> We evangelicals... are a conservative lot—conservative
> because we have something worth conserving. We don't
> change our methods and materials very easily because we do
> not want to tamper with the gospel itself and sometimes we
> are not sure just where the unchangeable gospel leaves off
> and the methodology of proclaiming it begins. In spite of our
> conservative attitudes we are affected more than we some-
> times realize by the rest of the Christian world as well as the
> non-Christian world about us.[1]

It seems to be the nature of church music to follow the
traditional path. By doing so, a large quantity of poor music
has been maintained in the church's repertoire. Recent ecu-
menical movements, together with the more extensive exposure to all kinds of music, have made many Christians more
ready to consider new types of music. In those congregations
where secular culture is not appreciated, church music tends
to stagnate. In many evangelical circles where musical tastes
are conservative, "conservative" means an addiction to specific nineteenth century or early twentieth century prototypes.
Furthermore, the conservative's tendency to maintain a musical style has frequently alienated from its ranks those who
are sensitive to contemporary artistic development.

Some evangelicals view the church more as a safe retreat
than as an opportunity for confrontation. Such Christians feel
that the church's responsibility is to gather people into the
local church. Although the Bible supports this, a balanced
biblical view regarding the ministry of the church must be
accepted before formulating a code of church practices, musical or otherwise. Those who regard the church as a retreat,
safe from the world, will have a tendency to think of all
values outside the church as corrupt. Styles and products of
earlier generations are frequently regarded as native to the
church, and the psychological power of association often wins
over the power of reason. Those who point this out will be
criticized, but history supports this position.

Evangelical groups have retained more nineteenth-
century-style church music than other religious groups. Few
have been brave enough to say, despite earlier associations,

1. Rockholt, "Creative Tensions in Church Music," p. 2.

"I would like to see what this new musical style can accomplish." Nearly always the response, "I don't like it," indicates a psychological resistance to music which is unfamiliar; the unfamiliar is usually disturbing.

In spite of their fear, however, some evangelical composers have recently experimented for the sake of communication. These have observed that evangelical church music has tended to preserve sentimental values, and are investigating what new forms of music will best serve the church in the future.

While some sacred song traditions should be set aside, perhaps some of the old ones which have been discarded should be returned. The recent urge to create and sing new material has caused many to forget older literature that can still communicate with freshness and relevance.[2]

Arguments for Pop-Style Music

In the earlier historical section (Part One) the church was shown to have often borrowed from the secular marketplace to find a "language" with which the man on the street could associate. In many cases, as this popular music was revised, it began to minister to the man in the church pew. Examples have been cited of the early church fathers in their attempts to fight heresy, the use of familiar styles of music by Martin Luther during the early years of the German Reformation, the use of popular music by the Wesleys in their revivals of eighteenth-century England, and the popularized texts and tunes of Ira Sankey in the late nineteenth century. This section deals with the statements and positions of current sacred pop music sympathizers.

Myra and Merrill write:

> The same kinds of tales could be told of Homer Rodeheaver, Wendell P. Loveless and John W. Peterson in the present century as they edge toward the sounds of the swing era and its big bands. Their new "special music" was

---

2. For additional information on pop music in the church, see the series of ten articles which appeared in *Music Ministry,* beginning in October, 1974. Each article is entitled, "Pioneers of Pop Ten Years Later."

scorned as "night-clubbish." Why all the flak? From the third century to the twentieth, the pattern is the same: church music gradually abandoning the ordinary man, leaving him without a ready medium for worship, and then some brave soul trying to fill the vacuum and get back in touch by writing music laymen can quickly grasp—and getting kicked in the teeth for it.[3]

A partial answer to the "new music" dilemma can be found as one recognizes the "two tracks" of music development and history. Music has always had its serious or "classical" track as well as its popular track. This has been true in the secular world as well as in the church. In recent years these two tracks have tried to merge. In serious, classical music, many of the idioms have left familiar tradition so far behind that a large segment of today's public has been alienated. This is one reason that so many people embrace the secular pop, folk, or rock music as "their" music.

Church music has for centuries had the music of the cathedral. But at the same time it has normally had the music of the parish church. Myra and Merrill further explain this church music dichotomy:

> The church has always been very big in the classical track, thanks to . . . Palestrina, Bach, Purcell, Beethoven, Schubert, Brahms, and other professional composers. Classical music is technical; you have to know some details to know what's going on. It is also *timeless* (or at least the composer hopes it will be!), made for all generations and centuries to appreciate.
>
> No problem there. But some Christians have also at times gotten into the popular track, the simple music of the masses. Here, techniques aren't nearly so crucial; most of the listeners know only that "it sounds good; I like it"—and that's enough.
>
> Popular music, of course, is very timely; its styles are constantly changing. It's throw-away music. No one song lasts very long; it's big for a brief period, then fades quickly into oblivion as something else develops. In rock, the cycle takes less than six months; in other genres, a couple of years.[4]

Today's sacred pop enthusiasts freely borrow evidence

---

3. Myra and Merrill, *Rock, Bach, and Superschlock*, p. 98.
4. Ibid., pp. 98–99.

from past church music history in defending their progressive position. William J. Peterson states:

> Isaac Watts, sometimes called the father of English hymnody . . . rebelled against singing the Old Testament Psalms. Indignantly, the older generation asked him, "Do you think you can do better than King David?" But Watts went ahead anyway . . . though he always was careful to identify his compositions as paraphrases of a psalm.
>
> When Charles Wesley began writing, he was asked, "Who do you think you are, Isaac Watts?" Wesley's use of some of Handel's melodies was criticized for being too worldly.
>
> Only a century ago, when Moody and Sankey went to Ireland, the catchy tunes that they introduced drew frequent criticism. . . .
>
> Most of the complaints these days center around the music, not the words. One of the main criticisms is that it is derived from the secular world, not from the traditional church styles. Weighed in the light of the history of church music, the complaint is absurd. Luther used the folk tradition of the Meistersinger as a model for his hymns. Moody could not sing a note, but when he saw how successfully the Catholics and Germans used music at their dances, he decided to incorporate more lively singing in his services.
>
> But beyond those tunes that are directly borrowed from secular sources are many others that show undeniable marks of being influenced by the secular music of the time. Church music in the latter half of the nineteenth century was strongly influenced by Stephen Foster. . . . If you study the gospel songs of this era, it is easy to see the resemblance. When Victor Herbert and Irving Berlin became popular, it wasn't long before their influence was felt in church.[5]

Advocates of the use of folk and pop styles in the church feel they have been "traditionalized" into a box and are unable to move forward and minister. They feel that those in the church who cannot accept the validity of today's folk movement (or any music which tends to be popular-oriented) are being inconsistent. They claim that the Sankey song was just as objectionable in the last century as contemporary popular music is today.

It is true that there was a difference between traditional

---

5. Peterson, "O, What a Fantastic New Day for Christian Music," p. 13.

and popular styles then, just as there is today, but it is difficult to tell exactly *how* different. Is the present use of the secular different today from previous use? Can the detractors of twentieth century innovation prove that it was different back then? In both instances the music in question was secular; each created a stir; each found a place in the church (at least in some churches). If the anti-pop crowd takes issue with today's folk idiom, it must take issue with the gospel song idiom also. But to do so is to criticize a form that has existed in church history for two hundred years. History has established its validity. How can anyone hope to prove that the gospel song is not an appropriate expression when it has fed and nourished a religious community for so long?

Don Hustad said,

> I recognize that we live perhaps in the most (as far as I know) frenetic, irrational day in the world's history. But, after all, we live in this day. This is our day. All expressions are man's expressions. They are not God-ordained. God didn't choose triple meter or duple meter to be worthy of Himself, despite all the efforts to prove otherwise. One generation says triple meter is like the Trinity so it is right. The other says triple meter is like the dance so it is wrong. All of this is man's idea.[6]

In many sectors of the church, religion and popular music have been enemies for years, but the popular track of church music continues to flourish. Some churches have been able to find a place in their ministries for a music which is both of and to the people outside the church. It is important that the Christian musical leader try to ignore his prejudices and judge music objectively, evaluating its merits and appropriateness to the need he is trying to fill. As Phillip Landgrave says:

> Every one of us has a sophomoric position that we arrive at, a time when we [think we know] what is good and what is bad and can put labels on everything. Until we get a little more wisdom, a little more experience, we are stuck with those labels and we stick those labels on everybody else's forehead,

---

6. Hustad, interview.

trying to indoctrinate and become crusaders in our ignorance.[7]

Often Christians accept the new sound when they are convinced that a particular piece of new music has an authentic
message for them and can be communicated, and when the
vehicle of communication is adequately learned. The
dynamic which makes popular music in the church a viable
idiom is its easy accessibility to volunteer, untrained singers
(which describes many of the singers in medium-sized or
smaller evangelical churches), giving them an immediate tool
for evangelism. If the music is well-prepared and performed
sincerely, it is more likely to be accepted.

We must consider the comments of some who have been
associated with organizations or movements long regarded to
be on the "classic track." As Paul Elbin writes in the periodical of the American Guild of Organists:

> It is my belief that current religious music in the folk-rock
> style is generally superior to the cheap nineteenth century
> gospel songs that were inspired by the sentimental ballads of
> that day. The simplicity and honesty of many folk-derived
> religious compositions surely make them more acceptable to
> men of good taste and religious devotion than the erotic "In
> the Garden" and similar musical aberrations of the past.[8]

Gordon Wakefield of the Methodist Church of Great Britain
wrote in the early seventies:

> In some ways, the last decade [the 1960s] of our fifty years
> [of hymnody] is the most exciting, since there have been
> attempts to break out of the traditional patterns of hymnody
> of post-Reformation Europe, to return to the style of medi-
> eval ballads, carols and Negro spirituals. Even where the metre
> and style are traditional, hymnody has become more aware of
> the world in which we live and of its urban culture.[9]

---

7. Landgrave, interview.

8. Paul Elbin, "Fanny Crosby and William H. Doane Have Had Their
Day," p. 43.

9. Gordon Wakefield, "Beliefs in Recent British Hymnody," p. 13.

Don Wyrtzen has experimented with sacred rock music, and even now generally writes in a style that shows a popular influence. This composer/arranger not only has had music training and wide experience, but he also holds a graduate degree from an evangelical seminary (Dallas Theological Seminary). His comments on pop or rock music should be considered by evangelical musicians:

> The form and the content must always be related to each other appropriately. ... Can rock music be used to present the Christian message? I have tried that and it is very difficult to do since so many of the forms in rock music are associated with totally non-Christian ideas. However, to be totally fair, some of the idioms of rock music will affect the total culture of which all of us are a part, and some of this is bound to filter into Christian music.[10]

Arguments Against Pop-Style Music

Many agree that witness music should be direct and simple. However, the detractors say it need not always be so. For, although the simple styles of the marketplace may be the easiest to assimilate, they are also the most difficult to shake loose from their secular moorings. For this reason, the church has normally let some period of time pass before borrowing, feeling that the longer the span, the stronger the possibility of dissociation from the source. In the past, this time was usually a period of generations or decades, but as the media of communication have become increasingly quick and effective, the waiting period has been shortened to years or even months. This is why Harold Best, one of evangelicalism's chief anti-pop spokesmen, can say that for the Christian, "the baroque dance suite is totally harmless, the Viennese waltz probably harmless, the panoply of jazz questionable, and rock highly controversial."[11]

Best goes on to ask the valid question, "Why must we commit ourselves so largely to retrograde creativity?"[12] It is a

---

10. Quoted by Robert Cook, "That New Religious Music," p. 8.

11. Harold Best, "There Is More to Redemption Than Meets the Ear," p. 16.

12. Ibid.

question many self-respecting evangelical church musicians have repeatedly asked. Why must so much of the music written for our use today be an obvious copy of the most recent "top ten"? Generally, creativity is a reflection of previous experience and training, but the amount of borrowing in the past ten to twelve years is alarming.

Even more distressing is the fact that the one institution which could best be trusted to improve the music (while still maintaining doctrinal orthodoxy)—the evangelical Christian college—is contributing very little. There are a few Christian college professors and church musicians writing musical witness material which is fully commendable as texts and styles designed for a particular locality. More of such material is needed. The church musician whose compositional ability is limited has a problem: he must depend on whatever is available from the commercial publisher. As is often the case, the publishing houses are concerned primarily with those songs and styles which are marketable.

Well, then, if certain musical styles are unacceptable, just what style or form *is* usable? Why does not the church-related college create effective witness music through creative projects in music theory and composition? No institution better knows the needs of the constituent churches, and at the same time knows the types of musical expression which best serve the purposes of evangelism. We need our colleges to create musical styles which are honest and acceptable, and in every respect uniquely the church's. It is inevitable that there will be disagreements, but as Best says, "if there is to be controversy, let it be one generated by a stunning authenticity."[13]

There are two consistent objections to the new styles of sacred music. First, there is the objection on matters of doctrine. This involves careful analyzation of the texts of songs used for witness. (Later in this chapter we will briefly examine conflicting theologies of evangelism [pp. 169ff.].) Second, there is the objection of matters of aesthetics. This involves careful study of the music and/or the text. (Since this is a study on the *music* of evangelism, not its theology, little space is given

13. Ibid.

to theological matters, except as they may influence the music.)

It was probably in the Wesleys' time that church music was first designated "good" or "bad" by those with aesthetic sensitivity. The typical Wesleyan tune used the secular operatic idiom to form an attractive melody undergirded by a minimal bass line. Wesleyan composers, in order to appeal to the illiterate congregation, often wrote "choruses," in which the layman would respond to a soloist. These composers also added repetitions and simple fugal sections to their tunes. In certain cases, Charles and John Wesley had some doubts about the new popular music, but the popular idiom continued, as can be seen in the subordination of the bass to the florid melody.

In this century, a few writers have commented on the poor aesthetic of much recent evangelistic music. Comments like those of Erik Routley regarding a respectable aesthetic even in music used for outreach must be considered:

> Music that is meant to endure, to be built into the continuing purpose of the church, needs that discipline, that understatement, that proportion and that prophetic insight that are the qualities of great art. . . . Music for ordinary people need not always be great art. It is a crime, of course, to exclude the possibility of great art from the church's life; and the best way to exclude it is to make people think that the perpetuation of transient art is the proper business of the church.[14]

Our heritage of evangelistic communication music assumes that the goal of the music is to reach the person without a developed artistic taste. Edwin Hughes, writing at a time when the light gospel song was most popular, quoted from the preface to Augustus Toplady's *Psalms and Hymns* which says, "God is the God of Truth, of Holiness and Elegance." He then went on to state:

> If only these quaint words could have been taken to heart, Toplady's hymn book would not only have put into circulation the greatest hymn, but would have prevented that per-

---

14. Routley, *Twentieth Century Church Music,* p. 202.

verse ignoring of the aesthetic side of human nature which proved such a serious barrier to the spread of evangelical religion.[15]

The sacred pop proponents would not support the petitions and warnings of the ancient Greek doctrine of ethos or more recent similar assertions that music, whether sacred or secular, has inherent moral qualities. To the pre-Christian Greeks, even rhythm was capable of producing varying kinds of responses. Those today who oppose pop music in church feel that music does have moral implications. John Morrison writes:

> Music (scale, rhythm, style, and so forth) is morally constituted. Although the advent of Protestantism wrestles away the formal censorship of the church (at least in Protestant lands), one cannot conclude that the church universal—Catholic and Protestant alike—did not continue to make judgments about "good" music and "bad" music. Out of the church, for that matter, music—secular music—has historically been viewed as producing either good or evil effects upon its listener because of its inherent nature. Good music makes good people and bad music makes bad people is the formula simply put.[16]

After citing supporting evidence from the Middle Ages, jazz in this century, and the *Oxford Companion to Music,* Morrison concludes:

> Any attempt to amicably blend the lyrics of the gospel with the despair of heathen sound would be morally contradictory and spirtually preposterous. Consequently, that would place gospel-rock groups in a precarious position: we would have the spectacle of profanity in God's temple without realizing it.[17]

Harold Best makes a plea to church musicians to begin creating and using higher quality musical art in the church and therefore fulfill their responsibility to give God only the

---

15. Hughes, *Worship in Music,* p. 81.
16. John Morrison, "Toward a Philosophy of Church Music," p. 49.
17. Ibid.

best. Unfortunately, Best maintains, the evangelical church today still has not developed a scriptural aesthetic of the arts, particularly of church music. In his opinion, much of the music of evangelism confuses beauty and truth with mediocrity and "results." He writes:

> Contentment with mediocrity as a would-be carrier of truth looms as a major hindrance to aesthetic maturity among evangelicals.
>   . . . Church music continues its round of habituating listeners to the comforts of the past and the third-handedness of the present. Just enough vestiges of classicism remain to impart a sense of history, and our borrowings are controversial enough to titillate our sense of contemporaneity. In confusing relevance with immediacy and communication with imitation we tend to reduce Christianity and what we call Christian music to a kind of competitive commodity.
>   . . . There are artists who reflect a new outlook: they refuse to view art as merely a "come-on" to worship and strive to avoid the use of art as a kind of cosmetic for Christianity. They have chosen to remain true to the surrender of their creative talents to God through disciplined workmanship.[18]

A musician not involved in church music is likely to consider many of the evangelistic styles very peculiar, or perhaps corrupt. It is apparent, however, that to a great number of musical evangelists the musical quality does not matter much so long as the job of communication and witness is accomplished. Best continues:

> We can use anything we want to in witnessing now. That's both a virtue and a vice. We're in this whole pragmatic mishmash that says, "If it works, it's good. If it'll bring souls to Jesus, it's good." As far as I'm concerned it's just pietized pragmatism.[19]

The recent borrowing of rock styles, for example, is probably an evidence of the loosening lifestyles in certain sectors of the church. Churches which have a concern for evangelism often conclude that the best way—if not the only way—to

---

18. Best, "There Is More to Redemption," p. 12.
19. Best, "Music: Offerings of Creativity," p. 13.

reach the man on the street is with familiar language. These churches then go about couching their witness in terms that the world is already using. The world invented these forms in the first place.

> We borrow it and give it back to them second-rate and second-hand. We choose what we choose because we want to massage and soothe people. We use music to produce feelings of warmth, comfort, and secularity. Then we load them up with the gospel.[20]

There are certain dangers in following this procedure. Some sacred pop antagonists feel that there is difficulty in trying to present Christian truth with methods that are "false." Confusion could result if a person is attracted to a new life through means that are a part of the old life. Whereas the pop proponents maintain that Christ used whatever means were at hand, even secular ones, for his use in ministering to others, the pop antagonists argue that we cannot ignore our priorities and violate artistic, biblical, or conscientious integrity for the sake of outreach. The antagonist would say that Christ *did not* forsake His integrity to attract an audience.

A common criticism is that too many churches attempt to mix entertainment with the important ministry of witnessing. This is a dangerous tendency, if not an utterly futile one. The average Christian group or organization cannot hope to compete with the world of secular entertainment. Erik Routley sounds a warning regarding the use of popular styles for outreach when he maintains that the "natural" in pop music is often corrupt. He adds that the genre is generally uncritical of music which is foolish, gaudy, unbalanced, and exaggerated. Pop music allows and inspires fantasies of magnificence.[21]

It would appear that the musician who uses sacred pop music could be on dangerous ground, for he mixes the gospel with the music of a morally loose society. In such a case, the musician has become the servant of an idiom, rather than a

---

20. Ibid.
21. Routley, *Twentieth Century Church Music*, p. 206.

message. Sacred music should not be entertaining, adds the pop music antagonist, since entertainment music is amusement which tends to steer the listener away from thought and reality.

According to Harold Best, there are at least three reasons why evangelism and entertainment should not be linked together. First of all, the associations with the secular, though they may be subtle, are entirely inappropriate. When it utilizes "entertainment evangelism," the church uses techniques and language which are determined by the world and by secular culture. The lower the aesthetic value, or the closer to cultural slang, the more one senses a compromise in Christian testimony. The church and culture are farther apart than ever before in history, and the less the church borrows from the world, the better.

Second, entertainment in the evangelical church has become more and more a matter of repetition. The church has unfortunately lost the ability to be inventive in perpetuating truth. The church considers music to be unspiritual if it is unfamiliar. Repeated entertainment music seems to be preferred because so little effort is necessary to understand it. No effort has been extended to replace it.

And third, entertainment music is largely free of spiritual commitment. Because it "describes without discerning" and "discourses without enlightening, yet satisfies," we must say that it denies a value system.[22] Best summarizes:

> If worship is mission, then the world will not see a reflection of itself and its amusements, but will be convinced that the church is a new creation and can produce her own means of expression in the strength of the Author of her faith. Otherwise music will be a gimmick of witness and will implicitly usurp the mysterious means and methods of the Holy Spirit whose way is final in preparing a soul for conversion.[23]

James Vail gives three reasons why the church should avoid the use of pop-style sacred music: (1) Pop music in the church becomes trite very soon; (2) pop music's reason for

---

22. Based on Harold Best, "Entertainment and Worship," pp. 5–6.
23. Ibid.

existence is strained when removed from its natural surrounding; and (3) young people are capable of being reached by language other than today's sacred pop music.[24]

A number of people with a background in secular rock or pop have come out of this environment and are now eager to share with others what they consider the dangers of this kind of music. Bob Larson, a former disc jockey, band leader, composer, and rock musician has become a Christian author, lecturer, and recording artist. In his writings and lectures he tries to expose the dangers of rock music, both in its secular form and in its use in religious circles. He claims that there is absolutely no place for "gospel rock" or for Christian entertainers to use rock music as a means for evangelism.

Larson also counsels against even a moderate position or approach to rock music in the church as an attempt to relate to the world on its level. Using his own experience and background in rock music, Larson attacks all forms of it because of the damage he claims it can have on a person mentally, physically, psychologically, and spiritually.

One of the strongest attacks leveled against rock music is against its rhythm and beat. The old Carl Seashore studies indicated that the more pronounced the rhythm of a piece, the more the intellectual powers of the listener decrease.[25] Heavy rhythm was said to contribute to a feeling of exhilaration, often bringing on a type of ecstasy and loss of touch with one's environment.

These studies may have uncovered some facts about the effects of musical expression, but these facts were very generalized in nature. For example, consider the type of musical expression which relates to bodily function, such as a faster tempo increasing the heart rate. High pitches are more exciting than low ones. These kinds of generalizations exist, but there is no intrinsic meaning in the music itself. Musical meaning is always within the culture, and it may even occasionally shift or change. However, Lee Olson writes:

> . . . one wonders how much real spiritual fruit has been the result of the so-called popular evangelism of today; if any, it is

---

24. Vail, "Values in Church Music," p. 10.
25. Carl E. Seashore, *The Psychology of Music.*

not a result of its music, but rather in spite of it. . . . Give heed
to the words of St. Augustine when he voices his distrust of
music from the fact that "the sense does not so attend on
reason as to follow her patiently; but having gained admission
merely for her sake, it strives even to run before her and be
her leader."

Rhythm is one of the constant elements in music most
likely to provoke a physical response. And when doing so, it
is not the friend of pious contemplation. The early church
recognized that fact. The evangelicals have forgotten it.[26]

Another strong indictment against today's rock-influenced
sacred music is that the high volume level of much of it often
obliterates the sole means of communication—the words.
Certainly no method of witness can be effective without
"language." And even laymen realize that exposure to exces-
sive noise is psychologically and physically harmful.

Antagonism toward popular-style church music has not
been limited to the Protestant evangelical camp. Although in
Roman Catholic circles the wide popularity of this music
indicates its general acceptance, not all Roman Catholics have
embraced it. One of the strongest statements opposing the
pop trend is by Ralph Thibodeau:

We have made two artistic compromises in our church
music: we have tried cheap vernacular settings of Mass-texts,
and vernacular hymns; and we have tried, in the name of
youth, rock and folk music.

As a result of the poor response of congregations to ill-
conceived efforts at having them sing, there has been created
in the church a musical vacuum. Into it have rushed legions of
litkooks, with priestlings in the van. With no knowledge of
music, and regretably, no real culture of any worth, they have
rushed in where angels fear to tread with their rock-and-roll
and manufactured-for-profit "folk music." In both congregational hymn singing and "folk" Masses, the rationale of the
incompetent authority has been to cater to the lowest common denominator, to "give the people what they want."[27]

The inherited forms of church music are not sacrosanct, for
they have been and will generally be in a state of flux. This is

---

26. Olson, "Church Music and Secularism," pp. 20–21.
27. Ralph Thibodeau, "Threnody for Sacred Music," p. 378.

true especially when it comes to music of evangelism, that music which is called upon to meet the man in the marketplace. The music in today's churches can be justified only as long as it meets the spiritual needs of the people to whom it speaks. Lee Olson states:

> Throughout the centuries the development of church music has never run smoothly, and in spite of the sincere efforts of the church fathers it was not free from worldly entangling alliances.... Throughout Christian history there has been a free interchange of music material between the church and the world.[28]

Perhaps some words of caution are in order. The minister of music with a burden for outreach must always strive to be discreet and appropriate for the good of everyone influenced by his ministry—those of his regular congregation, the mature Christian and the non-Christian. The music director must be aware that he is responsible to communicate with more than young people. Should he be successful in reaching them, he must know whether or not his music is alienating the orthodox, conservative Christian.

When selecting appropriate sacred music styles, church musicians must know where they should settle stylistically, after acknowledging the total Christian position. Integrity must prevail in every mode of outreach and witness, and in the challenge to be communicative to the non-Christian. Those who cannot get enough of the sacred folk and rock styles should be reminded of the following verses: "The fear of the Lord is the beginning of wisdom: and the knowledge of the holy is understanding" (Prov. 9:10); and "Be still and know that I am God" (Ps. 46:10).

Is There a "Sacred Music"?

Very early in this study an issue was raised which is often considered basic to the discussion of the place of popular-style music in the church, that is, the question of whether there is such a thing as "sacred" music. It is not my purpose to

---

28. Olson, "Church Music and Secularism," p. 22.

rehash the issue. However, recent developments in church music require a new, more contemporary consideration of this question. The following editorial appeared in a leading church music periodical:

> The "sacred-secular" illness is not a new one. Wherever the gospel has called people into that special community called the church, that community has produced a setting and materials for its unique functions. . . .
>
> But the question remains, "Is there anything *intrinsic to the music* which makes it sacred rather than secular?" To be specific are there "sacred" chords or chord progressions; are there "sacred" rhythms; are there "sacred" instruments, such as the organ, for example?
>
> We think not. Furthermore, concentration upon the "sacredness" of certain music (and the "secularity" of other music) is the chief reason we have a "sacred-secular" syndrome.
>
> Now it must be admitted that the church has indeed in the course of its life produced a number of musical styles which are recognizably "churchly" (or "sacred," if you will) even apart from any Christian words. Anyone acquainted with Western music will recognize a piece of plainchant or a chorale as being somehow "churchly." However, an uninitiated Oriental almost certainly would not.[29]

Many trained musicians agree that music has no moral significance in itself. Neither does it have philosophical or theological meaning. However, when a certain musical style or idiom is consistently used in a certain setting or place, it begins to take on the meaning of that place along with its context.

But it appears that musical laymen have a strong urge to attempt distinctions between a sacred and a secular style. They have every right to do this, of course; but generally their reasoning is based on emotional, even sentimental associations. Olson writes:

> There seems to be some confusion in evangelical circles in regard to what is meant by "church music" or "sacred music" or similar terms used to describe the musical literature of the Christian church. These terms have one feature in common, and that is, words and music, and that without text there can

---

29. "Church Music and the Sacred-Secular Syndrome," p. 40.

be no distinction between sacred and secular music. Music is neither religious nor irreligious. Instrumental music of a sober and devotional character, whether orchestra or organ or piano music, may be described as "churchly," but nothing else.[30]

During those times when the church is in need of renewal, the lines of distinction are most clearly drawn. It is then that revival starts and the church begins to look for new musical forms. Where do musicians go for these new forms? Outside the church, into the world, anywhere that they choose. Anything they utilize will be secular compared to what has been familiar for church use. It has come from outside the church so it is deemed secular, though it may be *potentially* sacred.

Music is a symbolic language of communication and expression. The meaning of music is less specific than the meaning of words, and is added by the culture in which it exists. It will, in fact, change from culture to culture and from age to age. In one, it will be secular and anti-church, and in the next, it may be pro-church. It is not absolute.

In 1971, James Vail acknowledged that "the blurring of any distinction between the sacred and the secular has been made almost complete in the last few years in the minds of many."[31]

It may help the person who is struggling with some of these issues to consider the fact that the Bible is not a textbook of aesthetics or musicology. The church, a supernatural phenomenon, exists alongside of music, a phenomenon now given to man to develop. Sometimes the relationship between these two phenomena has been a cordial one, while at other times it has been strained. The evangelical musician looking for some biblical authority to support the use of music in evangelism will not find anything very specific.

At the same time, some ministers of music may feel that their ministry must always be in and through great musical art. But the success of a musical ministry is not determined

---

30. Olson, "Church Music and Secularism," p. 17.
31. Vail, "Values in Church Music," p. 11.

by the stature of the composers listed in his weekly church bulletin, as these comments by Donald Hustad reveal:

> You are going to have real trouble if you take the standard from the world of pure art, because the serious artist, like the serious philosopher, can go astray; he can have sin in his judgment, in his perspective. You must evolve a philosophy of what church music is. You have to draw another separation in your own mind, between church music for what it is, and pure art. Church music has to be approached as a functional, instrumental art. It is not free. Great art is free; it must be beyond shackles. The art of worshipping God is not free. It is free only to worship God, and it is free to worship God in spirit and in truth and in its sincerity. It is in bondage. We must therefore approach the art of church music in terms of its purpose. Its purpose is to communicate and express for every [person] in the congregation.
>
> Music in the church being great art is irrelevant in terms of what the western world considers great art. You must pull yourself apart from approaching church music as a free art or as the best art. There are sacrifices to be made.[32]

Today's church musician would be wise to consider the potential dangers of setting firm lines of separation between "sacred" and "secular" forms of music, for in doing so he is likely to lose his point of contact with those outside the church. It is probably necessary to have some line, but it would be a mistake to have that line firmly fixed.

The Church's Search for "New Language"

One of the purposes of this book is to express the belief that although biblical truth does not change, the language in which that truth is couched does change. We have dealt with some of the facts, problems, and questions of a changing musical language. However, the musical considerations are but a part of a larger quest for new language. It would be helpful, therefore, to draw some parallels between the musical idioms and the new texts which are the real means of communication.

---

32. Hustad, interview.

Much of today's new church music deals with genuine contemporary issues. We have heard songs about war, ecology, and the rapture, all of which are not unrelated. Many of these texts show a new intimacy with Christ and a new familiarity with God—in some instances, perhaps this goes too far. Some of today's gospel lyricists should be reminded that God is God and that His chief attribute is holiness. On the other hand, many portions of Scripture speak of the Deity in familiar, personal terms, particularly in the Psalms. "The Lord is *my* Shepherd" (Ps. 23:1) or "The Lord is *my* Rock" (Ps. 18:2). He is also a friend that "sticketh closer than a brother" (Prov. 18:24).

Some are greatly concerned about both the music and the texts of the new music. To be sure, there is much room for the improvement in the lyrics, the part of a song which is designed to involve the mind and therefore the will. The problem of poor texts is not unique to our day, however. Just as doctrinal shortcomings occur in many modern songs, so doctrinal problems and tired cliches weakened many songs of the past.

The text and the sincerity of the composer and performer are what really make music "religious" in the end. Church leaders have a great responsibility to choose good texts, and the wise music director will choose music which will best allow the meaning of the text to be communicated.

The vernacular has a new meaning and importance in the twentieth century. This can be seen in the many new scriptural translations and paraphrases which have been recently released. It can be seen in the move by the Roman Catholic church toward an increased use of the native language. It can also be seen in significant changes in the texts of much of today's church music.

It is necessary that church leaders carefully analyze all texts, for at this point it is better to be critical than permissive. Recent cultural changes require that we state our beliefs in ways that do not suggest an ignorance of those changes. In our language, as in our music, we should not give the impression that we would rather have lived in an earlier generation. Indeed, the modern musical evangelist will function most effectively if his song is clear, based on Scripture, and associated with words and images that clearly indicate a contact with and compassion for his world.

The general content of evangelistic sermons preached a century ago may be similar to that offered today, but the homiletical styles have changed. Should not the Christian's songs of experience and outreach change as well? The struggle for an understandable language and a means for communication has been as great in the area of lyrics as it has been in the music. In some sectors the change in textual language may be even more significant than the new musical language. It is, after all, in the texts that one finds the significant specific religious expression.

Another whole book could be written on the changes in evangelical music texts of the last fifteen to twenty years. The imagery has changed, for the imagery usually relates to contemporary life. The concepts, the awareness, the feeling of conviction come from different images in different ways. The musical and/or textual language may be different (if it is to be effective) from one end of a town to the other. It might even be different across the street.

This section concludes with an example of an attempt to "contemporize" the language of the church in order to reach a certain segment of the subculture of the late sixties. For many years, one of the most effective means of personal evangelism has been the gospel tract. When I first read the tract quoted below, I felt it was ludicrous (I still do). Someone has felt, however, that to some person, somewhere, this was the best language to use in Christian witness. It was written in southern California in the late sixties, and it is titled, "Can You Dig It?"

I know you can dig that almost everyone today is hung-up. Why? Because you have been sold a phony bill of goods concerning reality. You have let the church "system" pull the wool over your eyes regarding who Jesus Christ really is. ... You get the idea that Jesus is some kind of a prejudiced, middle-class materialist or else some kind of a milk-toast character that wants to spoil your bag with a bunch of rules and regulations. ...

Jesus Christ is no namby-pamby character. In fact, Christ really socks it to you with some real heavy stuff. ...

Jesus said, "If you can dig on the words I have spoken to you. . . ."

Jesus Christ is truly the Cool One because He took the rap for you and me on the cross. . . . Even though we have all blown it, Christ died for us. . . .

Being a follower of Christ is truly where it's at. It's a groovy program, but it's not an easy one. . . .

Carrying your own cross means doing God's thing, not your own ego-trip. . . .

. . . If your bag is Jesus Christ, it's a heavenly trip all the way. But, if Christ is not your bag, then it's bad news for you because you're on an eternal bummer.

Jesus Christ busted out of the grave nearly 2,000 years ago; right now, He wants to bust into your life and make you hep to HIS program.[33]

Conflicting Theologies of Evangelism

This study has avoided discussion of evangelistic musical practices as found in sectors of differing theological persuasions, for two reasons. First, because this is a musical study, and a theological study would not be central to the topic. Second, I am not qualified to discuss doctrinal issues except to point out some of the differing musical practices which have resulted from these differing theologies.

The first doctrinal issue deals with the sovereignty of God. Arminians, or those who emphasize the importance of man's initiative in accepting salvation, tend toward the use of popular musical idioms in order to attract the non-Christian. Their music is more democratic. It is the music "of the people." The music of the Wesleys is a good example. Charles Finney (1792–1875) was a Wesleyan Arminian whose theory of evangelism put the requirements for revival into a formula: if God's people would repent, God would send revival—almost on cue. To Finney, revival could practically be programmed.

In contrast, Calvinists hold that God is sovereign in all matters, even in the actual process of drawing or attracting the non-Christian to Himself. The strict Calvinist therefore shuns any form of music which overtly functions as a manipulative device to bring a person to commitment. Such music

---

33. Rich Schmidt, "Can You Dig It?" Sunset Beach, CA., n.d.

would be totally unnecessary since God, through His Spirit, is sovereignly responsible for whatever "decision" is made. Calvinists throughout history have maintained a strict control of the musical styles used in their churches. There has been a centrality of and utter dependence on the preaching of the Scriptures. There have been no "devices" to attract the unbeliever; God will do His work with or without man's music. The psychological implementation of "the right kind" of music is not an important consideration for the Calvinist. Lovelace and Rice take this position: "A decision for Christ which is manipulated by psychological and social pressures— many revival conversions are in this category—is open to question."[34]

Some Calvinists, however, believe that the Christian must still be active in his witness simply to live in obedience to the command of Scripture. Just how many of today's sacred pop composers and performers have considered the theological assumptions of their music is not easy to determine. One must wonder, however, if traveling sacred pop groups, as well as the lay groups in the local churches, rely on this music simply because it makes them "sound good," in the same way the music from the secular world enhances its performers. Harold Best writes:

> Sure, the music gets people interested in Jesus, because that's the way we want to do it. I say that's not the way [we should do it]. We get people so culturally wrapped up in the faith that they are never really told what it means to be a Christian. People are lubricated into the church [with] the big evangelistic massage. Or the whole celebrity-loaded Christian television special. When you load mass communication with art, you must reduce it to its lowest common denominator. Ironically, you don't have to do this with preaching. It can be of the highest order and still hold people, because it's true. Not so with art. We've got spiritual Nielsen ratings. The market researchers are right; there's no doubt about it. It works, but I think that's the wrong way to evangelize.[35]

---

34. Austin C. Lovelace and William C. Rice, *Music and Worship in the Church*, p. 172.

35. Best, "Music: Offerings of Creativity," p. 15.

As a mood-setter, music can have a great deal of influence on one's thinking and behavior. A person can turn on a radio and in a short time find that his mood has changed completely. It is interesting to note how industrial and professional institutions frequently turn to Muzak for aid in increasing their employees' efficiency. In a typical advertisement from Muzak, one reads:

> The Science of Stimulus Progression—a productivity tool of contemporary management. Stimulus Progression is an exclusive concept of Muzak Corporation. Result of years of research and practical application, Stimulus Progression employs the inherent power of music in a controlled pattern to achieve predetermined psychological and physiological effects on people. Leading companies and commercial establishments now employ the Muzak concept to improve environment, attitudes and performance. Music by Muzak—when you want more than just melodies.[36]

The church must be careful not to fall victim to the kind of mood manipulation through music that has been recognized in today's business world. Evangelicals must make sure that the techniques of crowd control and human manipulation are not part of their music ministry.

Contemporary Efforts at Regulation: Dogmatism Versus Creativity

The Christian musician must be convinced that the contribution of his theological judgment to his musical judgment is essential. Theology is the science which should influence and inform all other sciences and arts. However, expertise in theology does not qualify one for musical criticism, though criticism can and should be based on theology. The best music for Christian use will be music which has been scrutinized by both the theologian and the musician, or even better, by the theologian/musician. The music must be doctrinally sound, as well as musically and culturally suitable.

---

36. *Scranton Tribune* (Pa.), August 11, 1973.

A number of difficulties have been encountered between church musicians in their attempts to witness through music and dogmatic, protective ministers. In the evangelical church, such encounters have been a significant cause of irritation. The ecclesiastics or theologians will disclaim, at one moment, any knowledge of music, but in the next they will make strong attempts to regulate the music used in their churches.

Certainly a minister has the right to expect the obedience and cooperation of all his staff members. However, decisions on musical policy based solely on emotion and opinion will usually cause great difficulty for the creative, progressive church musician. What is needed is a relationship of mutual respect, based on a free, open understanding and dialogue, under the guidance of biblical principles.

Chapter 9

The Music of Christian Witness Since 1970

A Broader Base for Evangelism

Most sacred pop styles introduced in the 1960s continued in the 1970s, as did the feuds between the proponents and antagonists of those styles. Several phenomena can be discerned which influenced witness music of the 1970s.

First, folk and rock music introduced electronic equipment to sacred music performance, giving even the most amateur group a feeling of power. The folk-rock influence also gave an emphasis on rhythm, rhythmic experimentation, and beat.

Second, campus movements and the so-called "Jesus People" used a very free musical expression, but often relied strictly on the words of Scripture for their texts.

Third, sacred music publishers experienced a significant increase in sales from the pop style, and they took thorough advantage of this in their advertising and promotion. The expanding recording industry instituted a new professionalism and commercialism. Today's church musician can hear a great deal of new witness music on big-budget record albums. Gospel music concerts with ticket sales are now common. Accompaniment tape tracks are available for choirs, groups, and soloists. There are awards and halls of fame for those gospel musicians who manage to survive the competition.

Frequently under the guise of Christian witness, the 1970s have seen a rash of new musical styles and experiments advance with incredible speed. For the cause of renewal or ecumenism, endeavors to reach out—historically limited to the ministry of evangelicals—have been carried on by those who are not known for their evangelistic activities.

In their desire to obey the Great Commission to be witnesses near and far, both independent and church-related groups have stepped up their efforts in evangelism. On the local scene this has resulted in the rise of church crusades and city-wide cooperative revival campaigns, coffee-house evangelism, beach evangelism, and street meetings. State-wide there have been various state denominational meetings and crusades in arenas and theaters. There have also been evangelistic campaigns on the national level as seen in Explo-72 in Dallas, Texas; and worldwide in the International Congress on Evangelism in Lausanne, Switzerland in 1974.

In the 1970s much evangelistic activity sprung from unusual sources. In a time of generally sagging memberships, the major denominations comprising the National Council of Churches took a very self-chastising look at their neglect of evangelism. Articles like the following were common:

> But not only the statistics, but rising pressures among rank and file members and unofficially formed blocks demanding more explicit work to spread and instill faith provided a backdrop to the newly signaled directions.
>
> The evangelistic task has been "minimized" among member denominations in recent years, with attention focused on rectifying social injustices,... echoing a criticism of many evangelism advocates.
>
> Similar reconsiderations have developed at the international level of the World Council of Churches, whose recent assembly in Nairobi, Kenya, put central stress on the urgency of propagating faith.[1]

---

1. "Clergy Shut Out by Laymen," *Scranton Times* (Pa.), August 31, 1976.

Even more recently has come this information:

America's major Protestant churches, spurred by recent declines in membership, are showing a renewed interest in evangelism, which they have long neglected and even shunned.

Among the bodies reflecting this ferment are the Lutherans, American Baptists, Northern Presbyterians, United Methodists, Episcopalians and Disciples of Christ, churches not considered aggressively evangelical in the past.

For the first time in two decades they are providing money and resources for evangelistic initiatives designed to strengthen the commitment of apathetic or lapsed members and to convert outsiders to Christ.[2]

Such churches have used contemporary music and art, modern dance, movies, slides, and plays in their services. The result has been church growth.

An important example of pop music being used for church growth is the work of Rev. Richard Avery and his choirmaster, Donald S. Marsh, of the First Presbyterian Church of Port Jervis, New York. One or the other of these men is usually on the road sharing ideas with church leaders who are seeking a similar growth in their churches.

With the arrival of the 1970s it was easier to discern the permanent from the ephemeral in new music. The Second Vatican Council (1962–65) provided a strong impetus for the use of folk songs in the Roman Catholic church. The continuing use of the guitar in the Roman church was assured, and with the Latin Mass translated into English, many Catholic writers responded with new songs in the folk idiom. These writers included Ray Repp, Peter Scholtes, Sister Miriam Therese, and Paul Quinlan.

From these few examples, one can see that practically the entire American church was affected by the popularizing of church music; the roots of the whole movement are those of today's culture. The music of the church is now more upbeat, more emotional, and less cerebral than it was for many years. However, musical styles became more conservative as the 1970s continued. It is what Carl Schalk has called "change in

---

2. "Protestant Chruches Show Renewed Interest in Evangelism," *Scranton Times* (Pa.), April 14, 1977, p. 21.

change."[3] He predicted that "this kind of change is likely to be revolutionary because it promises to be permanent."[4] He claimed that even in the early years of the 1970s the "pragmatic" publishers found fewer buyers of their material.

The music on most contemporary evangelical television programs is regularly in an upbeat style. The emphasis seems to be: think and sing positively; always be happy. Now we perpetuate these styles through our commercialism.

Music in today's church is more experience-centered. New performance concepts have been introduced through which the congregation is bombarded from all sides by many different media. There has been a movement to combine the arts for mixed media effects. There is musical sound; there are "visuals" (both slides and motion pictures); there is renewed interest in choreography; and there is a revival of church drama. In contrast to earlier years, many of today's creative church musicians do not try to avoid an emotional appeal.

The Commercial Market

Commercialism in evangelical music began in the late nineteenth century, when Ira Sankey and evangelist-composers were also involved in music publishing. But exactly what is commercial music? Harold Best gives as good an answer as any when he writes:

> Second-rate art has what one may call future inevitability: when experiencing it, one knows what to expect; he hears it "coming up." Its paths are familiar because the listener has been over the same paths before with other but similar works of art. . . . An alarming quantity of choral and organ music being published today evidences a questionable degree of sameness. . . . Quite often grammatical devices, structuring agents, are used as substitutes for structure itself and sound is sought rather than substance. Creativity is often thus surrendered to superficial contemporaneity.[5]

3. Carl Schalk, "Church Music in Transition: The Change in Change," p. 1251.

4. Ibid., p. 1252.

5. Best, "The Climate of Creativity," pp. 19–20.

In some instances, however, it is a curiosity that so many people label today's popular witness music as commercial. Is the use of popular music really any different from popular evangelistic preaching, or using the popular media such as radio and television? Today's ministers generally draw upon popular, everyday illustrations, as good preaching usually does. Is not a utilization of the familiar from popular culture similar to Christ's use of parables?

Perhaps the reason many people criticize commercialism is that the music style connotes a lifestyle and mindset which they identify as secular and even degrading. If that is a predominant perspective of a given community of believers, their minister of music would be well-advised not to re-create those experiences for his people.

But just who is responsible—the publisher, the composer, or the consumer—for the quality of today's church music? This question will probably never be settled, for when cornered, each points a finger at the other. However, Harold Best states:

> I can't help feel that much of the evangelistic witness phenomenon is tied up with financial outcome. When I talk with evangelical publishers or those who manage so-called Christian groups, they're very much concerned with what will sell. If a person's going to earn his bread by being a witness musician he's got to think of that. Granted. But I am offended by the theological and artistic concessions that are made to guarantee the bread.[6]

The Youth Musical in the 1970s

One of the most significant developments in outreach during the 1970s was the emerging of the youth musical. These have been, from the beginning, generally of an evangelistic nature. Many of the first musicals were musically poor and textually weak. In more recent years, however, a natural maturity in the youth musical has encouraged a more selective choice of music and text. The new works in the 1970s teach more Bible doctrine, and the audience appeal of the

---

6. Best, "Music: Offerings of Creativity," p. 13.

musicals has been increased to include children and adults. A new amalgamation of styles is evident. A large number of growing churches are using musicals in evangelism or religious education.

By and large, however, the folk musical is still the product of and for a searching youth population. It has brought many young people who might otherwise still be spectators, into an active, vital service group. Their new music is a tool of evangelism, as they sing in shopping centers, on the beach, on television, in coffee houses, and at youth centers.

A word of caution must be given, however. The number of musicals that offer good, sound training in doctrine is still quite small. Many works are popular with youth and even attract and help win them, but few of these musicals contribute to their spiritual maturity.

A problem which a successful youth choir must tackle, particularly if it is successful with musicals, is that of self-image. The musicals often are so well received that the experience quickly builds the youthful ego. Young people cannot always handle the applause. Phillip Landgrave, himself a composer of youth musicals and a successful director of this kind of music, analyzes this problem:

> They don't know how to deal with it. They want to label it "Christian enthusiasm" or something, but they begin to look and feel "superstarish." They begin to want to have sequins on their choir robes, more lights, more cameras, more action, more response. That is the pit they can fall into. It is the natural temptation.[7]

It is also important to realize that young people can sing more than just folk musicals. A steady diet of these will have deteriorating effects on the group's ability in sight-reading, sacred music appreciation, tone quality, and overall musicianship. A real danger exists in settling on the youth musical as "the answer" to all the young people's musical needs.

New Hymnals

In the turbulent 1960s and the early 1970s, during the time of the folk liturgies, a new type of hymnal was intro-

---

7. Landgrave, interview.

duced. Many denominations and church music publishing houses released their own editions of the spiral-bound hymnal; these pocket-size books were primarily designed for young people. Most of the books contained only a melody line and folk-style text. To encourage the use of a guitar or other chord-producing instrument, chord symbols were added above the text. These books, intended to supplement the regular hymnal of the church, were very popular.

During this time, says Carl Schalk,

> when worship in both Protestant and Catholic communities was largely up for grabs; when do-it-yourself liturgies and throw-away hymns were in; when guitars, bongos, handshaking down the aisles and CELEBRATION (always written in capital letters) were all the rage, other hands were steadily at work readying different kinds of materials which will probably be the more important shaper of what American Christians will sing in public worship in the years ahead.[8]

Some of the folk material found in the earlier spiral-bound supplements has been included in new hymnals which are likely to be more permanent. In these new hymnals, however, there is not an overabundance of folk material. Apparently, hymnal editors are convinced that the church has been exposed to enough of the folk/pop material. Schalk goes on to say:

> It soon became apparent that upon closer examination and with a familiarity born of more frequent use, most of this hymnody of protest and easy ecumenism was so questionable, theologically and musically, that it is simply fading into the oblivion someone has suggested it so richly deserved.[9]

Much of the popular material fell by the way because it was considered to be boring, and while the earlier movement toward popular hymnody created a greater willingness to accept changes, the song material that was first used was already beginning to lose its importance. Indeed, it is encouraging to

---

8. Carl Schalk, "New Hymnals: Shaping the Future of Congregational Singing," p. 5.
9. Ibid.

see in denominational and non-denominational hymnals alike an editorial commitment to the good contemporary tunes and texts. Tunes by such composers as Heinz Werner Zimmermann, Daniel Moe, Jan Bender, Carlton Young, Avery and Marsh, Ralph Carmichael, and Donald Hustad are more in evidence.[10]

The Worship-Evangelism Dichotomy

One of the strong, historical distinctions of the evangelical church is its practice of mingling the ministries of worship and evangelism. This has been true at least in most of the preaching, if not the music of the services.[11]

Unfortunately, the tendency exists in many churches to divide musical styles and intentions into categories of worship and evangelism. Many music leaders (and ministers as well, for that matter) place themselves in either the worship ministry or the evangelism ministry; they do not combine styles which could complement both. By doing so they prevent the people from experiencing the totality of worship.

A pastor spoke to this issue in a recent panel before a group of church music students. When asked how he divided his services in any given week between the ministries of worship and evangelism, he responded by comparing his services to a multi-course meal served in his home. He said that he would not expect his guests to keep coming back to his home several times in order to enjoy all the courses being served. Rather, all of the courses would be served at one sitting. This would not mean that each course would be in equal evidence, but each would be present. This was also true in the church services. In any season or service, the balance or emphasis could easily be altered according to the need of the moment. However, in every service, worship would be encouraged

---

10. See appendix for a selected list of some of the spiral-bound mini-folk hymnals.

11. One could point out that not all evangelical churches are necessarily evangelistic. In recent years it has become clear that a church can be evangelical in doctrine but not evangelistic in practice. In this study, however, we will continue to define evangelism in its broad sense, that is, persuading to action.

and promoted, evangelism attempted, and other elements of ministry would also be evident.

The following quote, however (by a member of the Pentecostal church), is an example of the philosophy and practice which characterize much of evangelical Christianity today:

> The fundamental difference between a worship service and an evangelistic service can be seen in the different general purposes of each. The worship service is usually intended for believers and is directed upward to God through prayer, praise, and thanksgiving in contrast to the evangelistic service which is directed outward toward unbelievers through witness, testimony, and challenge.
>
> Traditionally the Sunday morning service has been devoted to worship and the Sunday evening service to evangelism.[12]

The major problem with this practice, however, is that if the non-Christian enters the church at all, he is most likely to attend the Sunday morning service, which is the worship service.

This unfortunate separation has developed in too many churches. The dichotomy requires church service leaders to decide in advance whether the purpose of the service is worship or evangelism. This unnecessary division ignores the fact that the gospel can be presented in the preaching, the Scripture readings, and perhaps most important of all, in the singing of the congregation.

But church musicians must never overestimate the value of their work or ministry. There can most certainly be corporate worship without a single note of music, and there is nothing in evangelism which requires music. Music may help in these important areas of Christian endeavor, but the musician is being unrealistic if he believes that what he has to offer is indispensable.

There is no record of spectacular music having a significant effect in the evangelistic services of many great preachers of the past. If there was music at all in their services, it would have been the dependable, familiar Psalms and hymns of Christian doctrine. Ernest Pickering claims that evangelism will, in fact, come as a result of worship.

---

12. Delton Alford, *Music in the Pentecostal Church*, pp. 69–70.

Most unfortunately, a dichotomy has been created in the minds of many between worship and evangelism. It would seem (to listen to some) that a quiet, reverent worship service is . . . a deterrent to evangelism. . . . Were not sinners cut to the heart by the Spirit of God while sitting in the proper and quiet atmosphere . . . while Jonathan Edwards was preaching? What about the evangelistic fervency of Charles Spurgeon? Yet there were no special numbers, no musical extravaganzas such as are common today, and the hymns used were the great, solid, doctrinal hymns of the Christian church. . . . Worship must precede and accompany evangelism.[13]

Those who feel that an informal service, including "informal music," is the only kind of service in which evangelism can occur, should read the classic example of worship in Isaiah 6. The first four verses tell of the seraphim and their adoration and praise of God. They assumed an attitude of worship as they stood in His presence. They covered their faces and feet and exalted the holiness of God. An outline of the first eight verses reveals the basic steps inherent in any commitment or decision. Broadly speaking, these steps are:

1. *Adoration* of God (vv. 1–4). This is a realization of the character and nature of God.

2. *Confession* (v. 5). Acknowledgment of God's holiness will result in a feeling of utter unworthiness and will be followed by confession.

3. *Forgiveness* (vv. 6–7). The Scriptures promise that confession will result in forgiveness (see also I John 1:9).

4. *Decision* for God (v. 8). This is the step toward which worship is pointed. It is the desired goal of evangelism.

In this outline we can see that evangelism is part of worship. Christian ministry is not a matter of putting evangelism into a worship service or making worship a part of an "evangelistic" service. The two should be indivisible, evangelism being an outgrowth or result of true worship. Witness and outreach are involved in this scene of worship, as is easily seen in Isaiah 6:8, "Also I heard the voice of the Lord saying, Whom shall I send, and who will go for us? Then said I, Here

---

13. Ernest Pickering, *The Theology of Evangelism*, p. 59.

am I; send me." Cliff Barrows, the music director, song leader, and choir leader of the Billy Graham Evangelistic Association, writes, "I submit to you that music employed in evangelism . . . is one of the highest forms of music and worship."[14]

In this age of "easy believism," too many evangelists and musical evangelists present Christ and Christianity as simply another option to contemporary life problems. Too many songs have recommended Christianity because everything else (alcohol, drugs, sex) has failed. It is rather like trying on a coat in a clothing store; if it doesn't fit, take it off. But musical methodology in evangelism should follow the same high standards as the preaching. The music used should foster dignity and a reverence for God.

Many evangelicals behave as if they were married to a particular form and style of service. They assume that in order for people to be converted there must be a song service. But people can be converted in a normal service of worship. Historically, that was the common pattern in the church.[15] Christians today tend to confuse the idea of evangelism with revivalism, which is a unique part of American history. In the United States revivalism became a perpetual way of life, whereas in Europe revivals occurred only occasionally.

The church has lost sight of the importance of "total witness," a witness to the non-Christian world which testifies to the worthiness of God and the work of Christ. Speaking of this mission of the church, Harold Best states:

> Whatever name or form it takes, it must result from offering and nurture [which he has already defined as "growing in grace"] and must demonstrate to the unregenerate what these are like and how unlike them regeneracy is. . . . Evangelism is the church in action on the basis of the Great Commission and in demonstration of its offering and nurture.[16]

---

14. Cliff Barrows, "Music in Evangelism," p. 12.

15. Early church practice combined the work of worship and evangelism. See chap. 2.

16. Best, "Entertainment and Worship," pp. 4–5.

Certainly the validity of any "decision" is questionable which is the result of emotional and psychological manipulation or social pressure. The church must be honest in its worship aids as in its acts. In all things the evidence and ministry which are presented must say, "What you hear is the church and Christianity." One must question the ethics of using a popular-style music to gather and convert people, and then avoiding that style thereafter, implying that it is not suitable for worship. Stephen Hall elaborates:

> Then there were those who chose to use pop music as an attraction. They also faced problems concerning the ethics of their approach and the conservation of the immediate results. In addition there was the problem of drawing a line on how far youth would be permitted to go in their attempts to change the church. . . . Predictably it took only a short time for youth in these situations to realize that they were being deceived and manipulated, though sometimes with good intentions. For some an experience like this was enough to turn them away from the church; for others, although disappointed and disillusioned, their experience only convinced them of the need for a change in the church.[17]

In some sectors there has been a steady infusion of the "evangelistic-style" music into the worship service. Experienced music ministers agree that it is difficult to introduce a new style of music in outreach, and still be satisfied with the older, "status quo" sound of the worship service. Unfortunately, many church musicians subsist entirely on the older forms of church music. These older forms may help them feel secure, but is this rigidity healthy? Should not the emphasis be on balance between the old and the new? And, in the new forms, should there not be "popular-style" hymns and anthems of evangelism and Christian experience?

Harold Best warns of problems that result when a minister of music consistently separates his musical styles:

> One must also beware of the dangers of an impassable line of demarcation between Sunday morning music and Sunday night music. This division is caused by concepts that

---

17. Hall, "Christian Folk Musical," p. 41.

categorize music in such a way that quality is sacrificed for the sake of emphasis. Just as the preached word should be a changeless core of integrity with orbiting emphases, so must music. Perhaps the most serious challenge to the minister of music rests in accompanying the various stages of Christian birth and growth with equally fitting music. Music should be chosen, sung and played as if it were the only way to preach the gospel, as if the pulpit never existed.[18]

The process of integrating the musical concepts for worship and for evangelism is not easy. The seminaries would be the place to begin this integration, but many years would be required before the results would be felt in the churches. We need some adventurous, progressive seminary to gather its theologians and musicians with creative dramatists to see what might develop for the cause of Christian witness.

18. Best, "Climate of Creativity," p. 23.

Chapter 10

Summary and Conclusions

Lessons from History

Hegel, in the Introduction to his *Philosophy of History* (1832) has said that the only thing we learn from history is that we do not learn from history. Man is prone to make the same mistakes his forefathers made. This is why no presentation of history or a review of movements, cycles, or prejudices will settle the arguments concerning acceptable church music. Most issues related to musical preferences are too personal and deeply rooted in emotion to be dealt with simply by reciting facts.

Historic precedent for popularized, secularized evangelistic music has been cited, but many claim that the situation is different today. Indeed, in certain ways, contemporary activities are different from the past. But the church's concern for renewal has caused its musicians to turn to secular influences, as it did in the past, to find a vernacular expression for witness. Previously, however, there was less discrepancy between sacred and secular musical styles. Nevertheless, there are fresh and distinct musical forms available which are legitimate for use in today's church outreach. As Lloyd Pfautsch writes:

> The history of church music has recurring instances when the church borrowed from its environment. The church met the people where they were and appropriated what was familiar and meaningful to the people. However, it also distilled what it borrowed in such a way that the secular associations became secondary to the primacy of worship.[1]

Music continues to be one of the most effective media for transmitting the Christian faith, but it can only be effective as long as the musical style used is in the "language" of the people.

Some music ministers tend to forget the validity of the concepts of ethnomusicology in church outreach. Every culture has value simply because it exists, and popularized church music is a cultural phenomenon. We have tried to relate today's practices to other, similar phenomena in history, without bias concerning their validity. Recent interest in ethnomusicology has made it easier to justify this study today than it would have fifteen or twenty years ago.[2]

Much of our current sacred pop music stemmed from the non-evangelical, largely Anglican Church, which used popular music as an attracting medium for outreach. When it was suggested that those outside the church might not like the music, the music ministers changed it. The motive, whether it was evangelical or not, was evangelism—reaching people that the church had lost. For many years it had been idiomatic for the evangelical to use the music of the folk, but they were surprised when the liberals began to do so.

Certainly the styles of church music are influenced by the culture in which the church exists, and also by the music's purpose. There must be music for worship and music for nurturing and teaching. There must be music for testifying—music which is symbolically horizontal, from man to man, expressing personal thoughts about God and the Christian

---

1. Lloyd Pfautsch, "Worship and Crisis in Church Music," p. 5.
2. C.F. Robert Kauffman, "An Ethnomusicologist Looks at Church Music in the Seventies," pp. 3–4.

life. Finally, there must be music for witness and evangelism. Robert Cook writes of the varying music of the church:

> Each of these modes will reflect in some degree the milieu in which we exist; and each of these expressions should be done in musical and spiritual good taste, considering reverence for God whom we worship, and consideration for the fellow human we seek to win.[3]

It would appear that we are living in the midst of a sacred-secular merger. As stylistic homogeneity has been created and nurtured by lay people, so their music will be in familiar and popular styles. Church music must maintain some contact with the world, because the world needs the church.

In addition, there are two threads of development in church music. One is sacred art music; this is discussed by most writers of church music. The other is folk music in the church; this music has flourished more in the smaller parish church. The greater, classic music is associated primarily with the cathedral, royal chapels, and collegiate churches—when we speak of serious church music this is generally what we mean. The historic local parish church's music was largely congregational. The choir, if it existed at all, functioned almost entirely to assist the congregation in its singing.

The two traditions of sacred music are to be found in Scripture: the formal, professional music of temple worship, with professional instrumentalists and vocalists by the hundreds participating in a full-time ministry; and the spontaneous, para-liturgical music of the Old Testament—the music, for example, of the prophets (I Sam. 10:5–7), which was informal, amateur, and spontaneous.

The New Testament contains the same concept in the phrase "psalms, hymns, and spiritual songs" (Col. 3:16; Eph. 5:19). While the "psalms" and "hymns" were more dignified and premeditated, the "spiritual songs" were very likely wordless, ecstatic, and soloistic; improvised melodies created spontaneously in the midst of emotional Christian experience.

Those who embrace today's sacred pop styles as the complete answer to musical witness are in danger of making the

---

3. Cook, "That New Religious Music," p. 65.

192 / Witness Music Since 1960

same mistakes that were made with the gospel song tradition earlier in this century. To avoid these mistakes, the two lines of sacred music must be recognized: sacred art music and sacred popular music. As was said in chapter 1, the classical version of sacred music is that which became timeless, to be understood for years to come. But there is also the music of the populace in which technical matters are of less importance. This music lacks the durability of the sacred art form. Between the extreme forms of new music and "dated" music must be found idioms (one hopes it will be plural) which best meet the needs of those to whom the church musician ministers.

Determining "Good" and "Bad" Church Music

There have been times in history when the church viewed music as risky, which is understandable in view of the recent musical conflicts. This problem arises from the very nature of music itself; music is often emotional in its impact and its meaning is unspecific and unclear. It often produces a response which is impossible to counter with appeals to logic, examples in history, or even references in Scripture. That is why a person will like one style of music and dislike another style. He will ask, "Who says it isn't good music? I like it." He needs no other reason.

A chief criticism of contemporary outreach music is that it is bad music. One wonders, however, if some of the categories into which we have placed good and bad church music have not outlived their usefulness. The conservative church spokesman will claim that much of today's witness music sounds "too worldly" and not "churchy" enough. But this points out one of the most unfortunate problems of current church music—the notion that there is an explicit church style. This idea has kept many first-rate composers from writing for the church because they do not want to be forced into a style which disinterests them. They have a notion the "church style" is either too stodgy or too conservative.

So the argument continues over the values of secularization or contemporization of church music for purposes of outreach. There probably will be no resolution of this issue in the future, at least until churchgoers and church musicians agree that music should be dealt with on its own terms. On the other hand, it is probably not possible—or desirable—to separate music from moral issues, especially since music and morals today seem to be so inextricably bound together.

If it is true that only the best music is worthy of an offering to God, who determines what *is* best? The church must rethink this matter of authority in musical decisions. Too frequently, dogmas and policies are created by those who have little understanding of what church music is or could be, to say nothing of how to judge it or use it. A rigid authoritarian attitude toward musical style places unnecessary limitations on a proper judgment of the church's music. Robert Stevenson writes:

> By what criteria shall the greatness of a musical composer be measured? By the number of copies his music has sold? By the amount of recognition he received from important personages during his own lifetime? By the stir his comings and goings made in newspapers? And by what standards, more especially, shall we measure the greatness of a composer in the sacred field? Shall his worth be measured in such terms as these: numbers of persons who have been added to church membership rolls, or have responded to altar calls, or have visited inquiry rooms under the influence of his music?[4]

In order to mediate between the "music of the church" and the music of secular society, acting on the belief that musical styles are often difficult to categorize into sacred or secular, the church must find more music which is representative of the total music world. Too many church leaders claim allegiance to a single "church style" in music.

On the other hand, one may ask why it should be the church which must do the borrowing. First, secular culture has no reason to make changes. Its many and varied styles are achieving what they are meant to achieve, particularly to make money. Second, it is possible that the church, by instigating and perpetuating heated debates, is largely responsible for the existing alienation. Since the turn of the century,

---

4. Stevenson, *Patterns in Protestant Church Music*, p. 151.

evangelistic churches have been so dependent on the gospel song style that it has been difficult to separate them from it. This tenacious grip on a fading style has kept churches from communicating as effectively as they did in the sixteenth, eighteenth, and nineteenth centuries. Popular music changed quickly; church music changed slowly.

Here is a lesson to be learned. In church music which includes evangelism, musical barriers must not be constructed between the common man and the intellectual. The music of witness, just as a piece of furniture, may be completely functional even though to some it is aesthetically offensive. An artistic wedge must not be driven between those who love Renaissance anthems and those who prefer sacred folk music.

This is not a recommendation for a full-scale capitulation to marketplace/secular music, but for a broader base of styles to bridge the musical gap between the church and secular society. The most glaring error of the contemporary evangelical church is the error of judgment which has caused it to identify itself with a narrow selection of secular music—pop or rock.[5]

Music of Today's Church Outreach

It would be difficult to describe all of the new attempts at creating witness music in the last fifteen years, particularly since printed and recorded forms have been released so quickly. And it is as difficult to evaluate the effect of this music as it is to calculate the total output, particularly while the changes are still taking place. As Myra and Merrill state:

> Someday in 1997, a university professor can write an exhaustive recount of what really happened back there in the late 60s and 70s, and the truth will be known. Until then, most accounts will be lopsided.[6]

The revolution, the change, and the "change within change" are still too current to be dealt with objectively. We will not

5. For further material on the issue of authority in church music, see the four-article series in *Music Ministry* 4 (September 1971):4–11.
6. Myra and Merrill, *Rock, Bach, and Superschlock,* p. 107.

see, know, or understand the full results for years to come. Certainly many of the new idioms will find their way into our permanent repertoire, but it is too early to tell how many.

Witness music has been affected by the fact that we live in a multi-art, multi-media era. We are seeing the merging of many styles of popular music with styles of art music. Even rock music, which began rather simply, has become more complex and sophisticated. Cultural amalgamations have wedded together chant, rock, oriental ragas, and even electronic music to such an extent that popular art is less and less viewed as distinct from serious art. The success of today's pop music (whether within the church or outside) is due, in part, to the extreme, avant-garde movements of today's serious art. As Hustad explains:

> We are living in a predominantly democratic period of history and it is not surprising that our dominant music is a music of the people—jazz, pop, rock or whatever. [He also adds gospel music to this list.] . . . Music of today's serious composers, by and large, has lost its powers of communication and consequently its audience.[7]

The reasons for recent developments in church music are many and complex. Some are aesthetic; some, cultural; and some, theological. It should be obvious that the motivation for gospel folk and rock music is outreach. In the past, the greatness of writers of witness music was in their willingness to take musical risks. The problems inherited by evangelical musicians at mid-twentieth century were met head-on by emulators of jazz, pop, and rock idioms.

Many insist that these "trail-blazers" should not have borrowed these styles at all. Others claim that they should not have acted so hastily, but should have permitted these secular musical styles to lose some of their associations with secular lifestyles. Finally, there are those who believe that the new music is just what was needed. These claim that the rock, folk, and pop music were the natural expressions of the age.

Today's popular music is moving away from the extremes of the 1960s and early 1970s. However, of concern to many

---

7. Hustad, lecture.

is a trend away from Scripture, most quickly seen in the experience-oriented songs which rely heavily on personal feeling and emotion. This swing away from doctrine is serious, for success in evangelism cannot and should not be based on emotionalism. Experience is not to be a substitute for objective Scriptural truth.

In spite of disagreements in matters of philosophy and policy, there have been some benefits with the advent of new pop music in churches. Certainly more people have become involved in choral ministries than ever before, and certainly more people have been reached through a new enthusiasm in singing the gospel.

Still, problems remain to be faced and dealt with. The new music may help recruit, but it does not help the singer mature musically or spiritually. There is also a danger in generating an entertainment cult among young people, and in giving attention to the singer rather than the song, to the style rather than the message.

Advice for the Minister of Music

A time of revolution is not a comfortable period in which to live. A minister of music will hear cries of protest whether he is working with pop music or the new forms of serious music, because serious music also changes. Every effort should be made not to alienate either older Christians or younger Christians. The older Christian will remain loyal to the church; he is committed. The young person should be the focus of more concern—he may be lost if the music remains outdated.

The older Christian can learn to adjust his musical tastes when he sees how meaningful some new music is to young people. It is certainly better to have the young people up front singing worthy sacred folk music than not attending church at all. The youth must also be reminded how meaningful the traditional song is to adults so that "adult music" is not ignored. Ideally, both groups will be brought together in love, showing concern one for the other. The generation gap must be minimized. Besides, if we were to go back to some older style of witness music, just what would we go back to? Is there a perfect style? In matters of taste, change is inevitable.

Some people have difficulty accepting unfamiliar musical styles. In fact, this is one of the greatest problems a church musician must face. Just as he should not seek a single common musical denominator, in evangelistic activity he must search for acceptable styles which will reflect both the church auditorium and the marketplace. This task will be made much easier if the congregation has been fed a widely representative musical diet. The variety will eliminate the musical shock usually felt by both the congregation and those who are the objects of the church's outreach.

C. S. Lewis comments on the differences between highbrow and lowbrow music in the church, and the attitudes of highbrow and lowbrow toward each other. He talks about the grace given to the highbrow to endure what is meaningful to the lowbrow even though it is coarser fare than he would desire, and about the lowbrow who can silently endure the "finer stuff."

Lewis then wonders who we are to say what God likes in music. What are His tastes? Lewis's uncharacteristically careless answer is that if He wanted good music, He would not have asked us. The angels of heaven are His.[8] The trained church musician could respond to Lewis by indicating that God wants quality and deserves the best music—of any type. Certainly He wants good music, and He *did* ask us. A sacrifice—even a musical one—is most acceptable to Him when it has cost something. That cost may be in terms of money, possessions, or even time; time which may have been spent in careful rehearsal.

The generally artless quality of witness music today presents a problem to a person with a trained, professional musical conscience. The role of a dedicated musician in a church—that is, one who is committed to the task of spiritual ministry through music—is different from that of the professional, secular concert-hall musician. Concerning the church musician, Harold Best writes:

---

8. C. S. Lewis, "On Church Music," pp. 19–22.

He must be ready to empty himself in order to provide genuine help to his brothers. This emptying is not unlike our Lord's: the prerogatives of excellence are not preempted. Above all, he must be ready to make his music an offering. He must love his people deeply.[9]

In an earlier writing, Best said this of the church musician's ministry:

It must take its place alongside the supracultural impact of the pulpit ministry. The regenerate artist must speak to his culture by knowing *about* his culture. His mission is to be a prescriptive one, which grows from descriptive discernment of his generation.[10]

In his contribution to evangelism, the minister of music must try to balance the objectives of inspiration and order with that of meaningful witness. He must not become obsessed with church music or musical ideas—he must be concerned about *people.* Musical evangelism may require giving up musical pride. Sometimes it is necessary to make musical or textual concessions. It should not be, after all, a church musician's intention to impress people with his musical prowess, but rather to convince them of a need in their lives. The music which has been most successful in doing this has emerged from a specific, local need. Thus the local church musician should be encouraged to be creative for his community, and should also be understanding of those who differ with him, remembering that there may be several ways to achieve a goal. As George Stansbury writes:

A Christian believer has the right and the responsibility to proclaim his song! As a human being, man is capable of functioning in the role of creator and ideally, is free to express his unique creativity. Nevertheless, he must witness whether or not his creativity communicates to many or few. As a committed disciple of Jesus Christ, the Christian accepts the responsibility to witness *creatively* in the name of his Savior. Consequently, such expressions vary in style and form according to existing cultural conditions and relate to comparable

9. Best, "There Is More to Redemption," p. 18.
10. Best, "Climate of Creativity," pp. 12–13.

Christian testimonies only as witnesses to a common revelation of God.[11]

Church musicians must avoid the tendency to regard the means as the end, or to justify the means by the end. Rex Hicks states:

> Nevertheless, . . . the best organ, library, and church music equipment will not create an acceptable concept of church music, nor will they (in themselves) contribute anything toward the fulfillment of the Great Commission. They are a means only, and this is pure and simple logic.[12]

In this day Christian musical leaders must realize that Christian believers need both hymns of doctrine and songs of witness, both anthems of objective worship and folk cantatas of Christian service and discipleship. Syncretism may be difficult for the musician who has been conservatory-trained. However, he must select with care music for worship, edification, and evangelism, balancing the new with the old, the artless with the artistic, and the simple with the profound.

Donald Hustad offers advice for today's evangelical musician:

> Lift up your heads; forget your inferiority complex. The current pop-folk-jazz-rock phenomenon says to me that grandfather, Ira Sankey, William Howard Doane, B. B. McKinney . . . and in our day John Peterson, were right all the time despite our feeling of persecution and inferiority. At least, right for their time; at least partially right for their time. For part of a healthy expression of Christian faith and a logical medium of communicating it to others is a simple, folk art, experience song. And did I say that the Bible gives us no command to use such a song? Nevertheless it does record, it seems to me, that this kind of song has always existed in worship.[13]

The director of music must be sure that his musicians always minister in styles which they can perform convincingly.

---

11. Stansbury, "Music of the Billy Graham Crusades," p. 307.
12. Rex Hicks, "Common Sense in Church Music," p. 2.
13. Hustad, lecture.

He should be ready for the cultural shocks which may occur in the future, remembering that a leader cannot retreat into the safety of the past. He must not be ashamed of the old music or the new music if it is representative of the best. The director of music cannot simply imitate all idioms of the non-Christian world, but he should be sufficiently aware of them to utilize some of them for his own honorable purpose.

He should work toward a balance, for balance encourages personal growth. He should continue, to some extent, the popular styles, but in a two-track phase. He will always need music which is accessible to those with limited experience, since one of the main values of the new popular style has been its use as an enlistment tool. A second track needs to be followed, not just with sophisticated music, but also with texts which will promote maturity. Young and old alike must be taught that if they are going to adequately edify and praise, their music must allow other people to vicariously and personally praise God.

The minister of music must see himself as an evangelist in several areas of his ministry—in his building of a graded choir system as a contribution to building the church; in attracting young people with the use of youth-oriented music; in selecting worship music which presents truth in its text and quality; in selecting songs of both Christian experience and objective expressions of praise; and in developing smaller, evangelistic groups for musical witness outside the church.

Finally, the church musician must remember the most important music ministry of his church, the music of the congregation. An evangelistic church is generally a singing church. Hearty singing has accompanied great revival periods in the past, and the music director should earnestly desire this same experience for his congregation.

Predictions

Far-reaching predictions for the direction—or directions—of Christian witness music are difficult to make. Since this music is a reflection of the cultural, philosophical, and theological positions of the time in which it was created, it might be easier to look to the sociologist, artist, philosopher, or theologian for insights to the future.

It is safe to assume, however, that many of the idioms used for outreach will merge with other forms of worship music, just as new styles have done in the past. This music will very likely remain in the church until another movement of renewal or revival brings in its own forms and idioms. The 1970s were a part of a larger romantic movement whose emphasis was away from the objective and rational and toward an experience-oriented music and lyric. It is impossible to determine how long this movement will last.

While some churches will cling to their favorite musical tradition, others will broaden their stylistic base. Right or wrong, some churches may even have a virtual musical potpourri, a full eclectic experience in the services, with the music of Deprès, Bach, Brückner, Sankey, Daniel Pinkham, and various sacred pop musicians all receiving credit in the worship bulletin from time to time.

If expression is given to the totality of American religious expression, there will certainly be a place for the gospel song. We will also see more of the "guitar-plucking kids who play three bad chords but smile a lot (while we hold our ears and cry, 'How long, O Lord!')."[14]

Carlton Young predicted that we are moving toward "a wider acceptance of an American style of church music—a style both instrumental and vocal, both choral and congregational. . . ."[15]

It could be that the musical evangelists of the last fifteen years were prophets all along. As we look forward to the use of music in the work of Christian outreach, we can be certain that new musical expressions will be accompanied by conflicts in attitude and philosophy, and we can be equally certain that these new idioms will be necessary.

---

14. Carlton Young, "Church Music, American Style: What's Ahead?" p. 8.
15. Ibid., p. 11.

Appendix

A Selected List of Extended Works
Folk Hymnals

Contemporary Popular Idioms in Church Music

SECTION ONE

A Selected List of Extended Works

Folk Musicals (Non-Seasonal)

Composer	Title	Publisher
Adair, Tom & Frances & Hammack, Bob	I Want You	Lexicon
Adams, J. T.	Time Out	Sacred Songs
Burkum, Lowell & David	Let Him Shine on You	Lillenas
Burroughs, Bob	Now Hear It Again	Broadman
Carmichael-Kaiser	I'm Here, God's Here, Now We Can Start	Lexicon
Carmichael-Kaiser	Natural High	Sacred Songs
Carmichael-Kaiser	Tell It Like It Is	Sacred Songs
Fischer, John	The New Covenant	Lexicon
Floria, Cam	Share	Lexicon
Gagliardi, George	A New Kind of Dream	Fine Arts
Gassman, Clark	The Word Made Music	Lexicon
Hawkins-Skillings	Discovery	Lillenas

Hustad, Don	Celebration of Discipleship	Hope
Johnson-Skillings	A Celebration of Hope	Lillenas
Johnson, Paul	Here Comes The Son	Word
Johnson, Paul	Sonlife	Lillenas
Krogstad-Wyrtzen	Love Was When— Love Is Now	Singspiration
Landgrave, Phillip	Christ in You the Hope	Hope
Landgrave, Phillip	Involvement	Manuscript
Landgrave, Phillip	Purpose	Broadman
Martin, Gilbert	Now!	Lorenz
Medema, Ken	Moses	Word
Skillings-Owens	The Carpenter	Benson
Nichols, Ted	He Is Forever	Praise Music (Gospel Light)
Nichols, Ted	Opus for Contemporary Decision	Hope
Oldenburg, Bob	Good News	Broadman
Oldenburg, Bob	Happening Now	Broadman
Oldenburg-Allen	Real	Lexicon
Red, Buryl	Hello World	Broadman
Salsbury, Sonny	Backpacker's Suite	Word
Skillings, Otis	Jesus Is Lord	Lillenas
Skillings, Otis	Life	Lillenas
Skillings, Otis	Love	Lillenas
Smith, Tedd	New Vibrations	Lexicon
Smolover	Where the Rainbow Ends	Belwin Mills
Wilson, John	Man Alive!	Hope
Wyrtzen, Don	Breakthrough	Singspiration
Wyrtzen, Don	What's It All About Anyhow?	Zondervan

Folk Musicals (Seasonal)

Composer	Title	Publisher
Mayfield, Larry	Can It Be? (Easter)	Lillenas
Mayfield, Larry	Get Ready! (Christmas)	Lillenas
Oldenburg, Bob	A Song of Life	Broadman
Salsbury, Sonny	Love Came Down (Christmas)	Word

Smith, Lani	It's the Lord's Thing	Lorenz
Wilson, John	A Christmas Happening	Hope
Wilson, John	I Believe He's the Son of God	Hope
Wilson, John	Shepherds, Rejoice	Hope

Children's Folk Musicals

Hurd, Michael	Jonah-Man Jazz	Marks
Chappell, Herbert	The Daniel Jazz	Marks
Lloyd-Chappell	The Christmas Jazz	Marks
Lloyd-Chappell	The Goliath Jazz	Marks
Lloyd-Chappell	The Jericho Jazz	Marks
Lloyd-Chappell	The Noah Jazz	Marks
Lloyd-Chappell	The Prodigal Son Jazz	Marks
Lloyd-Chappell	The Red Sea Jazz	Marks
Price, Flo	And That's the Truth	Lexicon
Turner, Lee & Dianne	They All Sang Jesus!	Benson

Music Dramas

Composer	Title	Publisher
Burroughs, Bob	In My Father's Name	Sunshine Prod. (Lorenz)
Cook, Rich	Living Witnesses	Benson
Landgrave, Phillip	Living in the Spirit	Broadman
Mays, Carl	The Clown	Benson
Red, Buryl	Lightshine!	Word
Seabough, Ed & Burroughs, Bob	The Call of God	Lillenas
Silver-Kromer	For Heaven's Sake	Baker's Plays
Silver-Kromer	Like It Is	Baker's Plays
Wells, Ronald	I Wonder	Crescendo
Wells, Ronald	Who Is My Neighbor?	Crescendo

Oratorios

Brubeck, Dave	The Light in the Wilderness	Shawnee
Floria, Cam	It's Getting Late	Lexicon
Murray, Don	Seeds of Contemplation	Manuscript

Services

Landgrave, Phillip	The Walls	Manuscript
Myers, Richard	Celebration	Manuscript

| Owens, Jimmy & Carol | If My People | Lexicon |

Contemporary Popular Idioms in Church Music

Masses

Composer	Title	Publisher
Beaumont, Geoffrey	20th Century Folk Mass	Weinberger
Bonnemere, Edward	Missa Laetare	Lutheran Church
Draessel, Herbert	Celebration	Marks
Draessel, Herbert	Rejoice	Marks
Electric Prunes	Mass in F	
Ramirez, Ariel	Misa Criolla	G. Schirmer
Schiffrin, Lalo	Jazz Suite on Mass Texts	
Summerlin, Edgar	Requiem for Mary Jo	Summerlin
Tirro, Frank P.	American Jazz Mass	Summy-Birchard
Winter, Miriam Therese	Mass of a Pilgrim People	Vanguard

SECTION TWO

Folk Hymnals

Title	Publisher
Alleluia: Hymnbook for Inner-City Parishes	Cooperative Recreation Service, Inc. (Delaware, Ohio)
A New Now	Hope
Dunblane Praises No. 1 & 2	Scottish Churches' House (Dunblane, Perthshire)
Folk Encounter	Hope
The Genesis Songbook	Agape (Hope)
Gospel Song Book	Geoffrey Chapman, LTD (London)
He's Everything to Me plus 153	Lexicon
Hymnal for Young Christians	F.E.L. Church Publishers
Lift Him Up	Benson
Lord of Reality	Tyndale House Publishers
Scripture Sings	New Life Publications

Scriptures to Sing	Lillenas
Shiloh	Word
Sing 'n' Celebrate	Word
Sing In	Sacred Songs
Songbook for Saints and Sinners	Agape (Hope)

Bibliography

Books

Alford, Delton. *Music in the Pentecostal Church*. Cleveland, Tenn.: Pathway Press, 1967.

Allen, Cecil J. *Hymns and the Christian Faith*. London: Pickering and Inglis, 1966.

Allen, Warren Dwight. *Philosophies of Music History*. New York: Dover Publications, 1939.

Apel, Willi. *Harvard Dictionary of Music*. 2d rev. ed. Cambridge: Harvard University Press, 1969.

Ashton, Joseph. *Music in Worship*. Boston: Pilgrim Press, 1943.

Bailey, Albert E. *The Gospel in Hymns: Backgrounds and Interpretations*. New York: Charles Scribner's Sons, 1950.

Basil. *Exegetic Homilies*. Translated by Agnes Clare Way. Washington, D.C.: The Catholic University of America Press, 1963.

Benson, Louis F. *The English Hymn: Its Development and Use in Worship*. New York: George H. Doran, 1915; reprint ed., Richmond, Va.: John Knox Press, 1962.

_____. *The Hymnody of the Christian Church*. New York: George H. Doran, 1927; reprint ed., Richmond, Va.: John Knox Press, 1956.

Blankenburg, Walter. "Church Music in Reformed Europe." In

Protestant Church Music, edited by Friedrich Blume. New York: W. W. Norton, 1974.

Blackwood, Andrew W. *The Fine Art of Public Worship.* New York: Abingdon Cokesbury Press, 1939.

Blume, Friedrich. *Protestant Church Music.* New York: W. W. Norton, 1974. (Various translators.)

Blume, Friedrich. *Renaissance and Baroque Music.* Translated by Herter Norton. New York: W. W. Norton, 1967.

Borroff, Edith. *Music in Europe and the United States.* Englewood Cliffs, N.J.: Prentice-Hall, 1971.

Breed, David Riddle. *The History and Use of Hymns and Hymn-tunes.* Chicago: Fleming H. Revell, 1903.

Buchanan, Annabel Morris. *Folk Hymns of America.* New York: J. Fischer and Bro., 1938.

Bukofzer, Manfred F. *Music in the Baroque Era.* New York: W. W. Norton, 1947.

Burney, Charles. *A General History of Music.* Originally published by the author, 1789; reprint ed., New York: Dover Publications, 1957.

Chase, Gilbert. *America's Music: From the Pilgrims to the Present.* Rev. 2nd ed. New York: McGraw-Hill, 1966.

Coulton, G. G. *Art and the Reformation.* Hamden, Conn.: Archon Books, 1969, reprint of the 1928 edition.

Crocker, Richard L. *A History of Musical Style.* New York: McGraw-Hill, 1966.

Davison, Archibald T. *Protestant Church Music in America.* Boston: E. C. Schirmer, 1933.

―――. *Church Music: Illusion and Reality.* Cambridge: Harvard University Press, 1952.

Davison, Archibald T., and Apel, Willi, eds. *Historical Anthology of Music.* Vol. 1. Cambridge: Harvard University Press, 1949.

Day, Richard Ellsworth. *Bush Aglow.* Philadelphia: Judson Press, 1936.

Dickinson, Edward. *Music in the History of the Western Church.* New York: Charles Scribner's Sons, 1902.

Dorian, Frederick. *The History of Music in Performance.* New York: W. W. Norton, 1942.

Douglas, Winfred. *Church Music in History and Practice.* New York: Charles Scribner's Sons, 1962.

Ellinwood, Leonard. *History of American Church Music.* New York: Morehouse-Gorham, 1953.

Ellis, William T. *Billy Sunday.* Chicago: Moody Press, 1959.

Elson, Louis. *History of American Music.* New ed., revised by Arthur Elson. New York: Burt Franklin, 1971.

Escott, Harry. *Isaac Watts, Hymnographer.* London: Independent Press, 1962.

Etherington, Charles L. *Protestant Worship Music.* New York: Holt, Rinehart & Winston, 1962.

Fleming, George T. *The Music of the Congregation.* London: Faith Press, 1923.

Foote, Henry Wilder. *Three Centuries of American Hymnody.* Cambridge: Harvard University Press, 1940.

Green, Joseph F. *Biblical Foundations for Church Music.* Nashville: Convention Press of the Southern Baptist Convention, 1967.

Green, Michael. *Evangelism in the Early Church.* Grand Rapids: William B. Eerdmans, 1970.

Grout, Donald Jay. *A History of Western Music.* New York: W. W. Norton, 1960; rev. ed., 1973.

Halter, Carl. *The Practice of Sacred Music.* St. Louis: Concordia Publishing House, 1955.

Headley, P. C. *Evangelists in the Church from Philip to Moody and Sankey.* Boston: Henry Hoyt, 1875.

Heyer, Robert, ed. *Discovery in Song.* New York: Association Press, 1968.

Howard, John Tasker. *Our American Music.* New York: Thomas Crowell, 1954.

Hughes, Edwin Holt. *Worship in Music.* Nashville: Abingdon Press, 1929.

Jackson, George Pullen. *Spiritual Folk-Songs of Early America.* New York: Augustin Publishers, 1953.

Jasper, Tony. *Jesus in a Pop Culture.* Glasgow: Fontana Books, 1975.

Jones, Ilion T. *A Historical Approach to Evangelical Worship.* Nashville: Abingdon, 1954.

Julian, John. *A Dictionary of Hymnology.* London: J. Murray, 1907; reprint ed. New York: Dover Publications, 1957.

Kerr, Phil. *Music in Evangelism.* 5th ed. Glendale, CA.: Gospel Music Publishers, 1959.

Lang, Paul Henry. *Music in Western Civilization.* New York: W. W. Norton, 1941.

Larson, Bob. *Rock and the Church.* Carol Stream, Ill.: Creation House, 1971.

Latourette, Kenneth S. *A History of the Expansion of Christianity.* New York: Harper and Bros., 1937.

————. *History of Christianity.* New York: Harper and Bros., 1953.

Leichtentritt, Hugo. *Music, History and Ideas.* Cambridge: Harvard University Press, 1947.

Liemohn, Edwin. *The Chorale through 400 Years of Musical Development as a Congregational Hymn.* Philadelphia: Muhlenberg Press, 1953.

Lovelace, Austin C. *Anatomy of Hymnody.* Nashville: Abingdon Press, 1965.

Lovelace, Austin C., and Rice, William C. *Music and Worship in the Church.* Rev. ed. Nashville: Abingdon Press, 1976.

Manning, Bernard Lord. *The Hymns of Wesley and Watts.* London: Epworth Press, 1942.

Marks, Harvey B. *The Rise and Growth of English Hymnody.* Old Tappan, N.J.: Fleming H. Revell, 1938.

Martin, Ralph P. *Worship in the Early Church.* Grand Rapids: William B. Eerdmans, 1964.

McCutchan, Robert Guy. *Hymns in the Lives of Men.* Nashville: Abingdon-Cokesbury Press, 1945.

McNaugher, John, ed. *The Psalms in Worship.* Pittsburgh: United Presbyterian Board of Publication, 1907.

Messenger, Ruth Ellis. *The Medieval Latin Hymn.* Washington, D.C.: Capital Press, 1953.

Miller, William R. *The Christian Encounters the World of Pop Music and Jazz.* St. Louis: Concordia Publishing House, 1965.

Myra, Harold, and Merrill, Dean. *Rock, Bach, and Superschlock.* Philadelphia: J. B. Lippincott, 1972.

Ninde, Edward S. *Nineteen Centuries of Christian Song.* Old Tappan, N.J.: Fleming H. Revell, 1938.

Oesterley, W. D. E. *The Jewish Background of the Christian Liturgy.* London: Oxford University Press, 1925.

Patrick, Millar. *The Story of the Church's Song.* Richmond, Va.: John Knox Press, 1962.

Peck, Ira, ed. *The New Sound, Yes!* New York: The Four Winds Press, 1966.

Pickering, Ernest. *The Theology of Evangelism.* Clarks Summit, Pa.: Baptist Bible College Press, 1974.

Pratt, Waldo Selden. *The Music of the French Psalter of 1562.* New York: Columbia University Press, 1939.

Pritchard, Constantine E., and Bernard, Edward R., eds. *Selected Letters of Pliny.* Oxford: Clarendon Press, 1891.

Reese, Gustave. *Music in the Middle Ages.* New York: W. W. Norton, 1940.

_____. *Music in the Renaissance.* Rev. ed. New York: W. W. Norton, 1959.

Reynolds, William J. *A Survey of Christian Hymnody.* New York: Holt, Rinehart & Winston, 1963.

Riedel, Johannes. *The Lutheran Chorale: Its Basic Tradition.* Minneapolis: Augsburg Publishing House, 1967.

Robertson, Alec. *Sacred Music.* New York: Chanticleer Press, 1950.

_____. *Christian Music.* New York: Hawthorne Books, 1961.

Rodeheaver, Homer. *Twenty Years with Billy Sunday.* Winona Lake, Ind.: The Rodeheaver Hall-Mack Co., 1935.

Routley, Erik. *The Church and Music.* Chester Springs, Pa.: Dufour Editions, 1952.

_____. *Hymns and Human Life.* London: John Murray, 1952.

_____. *Hymns and the Faith.* London: John Murray, 1955.

_____. *The Music of Christian Hymnody.* London: Independent Press, 1957.

_____. *The English Carol.* London: Oxford University Press, 1958.

_____. *Church Music and Theology.* Philadelphia: Muhlenberg Press, 1959.

_____. *Music, Sacred and Profane.* London: Independent Press, 1960.

_____. *Hymns Today and Tomorrow.* Nashville: Abingdon Press, 1964.

_____. *Twentieth Century Church Music.* London: Herbert Jenkins, 1964.

_____. *Music Leadership in the Church.* Nashville: Abingdon Press, 1967.

_____. *The Musical Wesleys.* New York: Oxford University Press, 1968.

_____. *Words, Music and the Church.* Nashville: Abingdon Press, 1968.

Ryden, E. E. *The Story of Christian Hymnody.* Rock Island, Ill.: Augustana Press, 1959.

Sankey, Ira D. *My Life and the Story of the Gospel Hymns.* New York: AMS Press, 1974.

Savary, Louis M. *The Kingdom of Downtown.* New York: Paulist Press, 1967.

Schafer, William J. *Rock Music: Where It's Been, What It Means, Where It's Going.* Minneapolis: Augsburg Publishing House, 1972.

Scharpff, Paulus. *History of Evangelism.* Translated by Helga Bender Henry. Grand Rapids: William B. Eerdmans, 1966.

Seashore, Carl E. *The Psychology of Music.* New York: McGraw-Hill, 1938.

Schrade, Leo. *Bach: The Conflict between the Sacred and the Secular.* New York: Da Capo Press, 1955.

Stevenson, Arthur L. *The Story of Southern Hymnology.* New York: AMS Press, 1931.

Stevenson, Robert M. *Patterns in Protestant Church Music.* Durham, N.C.: Duke University Press, 1953.

———. *Protestant Church Music in America.* New York: W. W. Norton, 1966.

Sweet, William Warren. *Revivalism in America.* New York: Charles Scribner's Sons, 1944.

Terry, Harold. *Leader's Guide to Folk Music in Today's Church.* Impact Series. Philadelphia: Lutheran Church Press, 1971.

Thomson, S. Harrison. *Europe in Renaissance and Reformation.* New York: Harcourt, Brace and World, 1963.

Topp, Dale. *Music in the Christian Community.* Grand Rapids: William B. Eerdmans, 1976.

Wellesz, Egon. *Eastern Elements in Western Chant.* Oxford: Byzantine Institute, 1947.

———. *A History of Byzantine Music and Hymnography.* 2nd ed. Oxford: Clarendon Press, 1961.

Werner, Eric. *The Sacred Bridge.* New York: Columbia University Press, 1959.

Wienandt, Elwyn. *Choral Music of the Church.* New York: Free Press, 1965.

———, ed. *Opinions on Church Music.* Waco, Taxas: Baylor University Press, 1974.

Wilson, Archibald W. *The Chorales, Their Origin and Influence.* London: The Faith Press, 1920.

Wohlgemuth, Paul W. *Rethinking Church Music.* Chicago: Moody Press, 1973.

Wood, J. "Reflections on the Nature of Jazz." In *Jazzbook,* edited by A. J. McCarthy. London: Cassell, 1955.

Wright, Thomas. *Isaac Watts and Contemporary Hymn-Writers.* London: C. J. Faircombe and Sons, 1914.

Periodicals

Baker, Robert. "Shall We Quit, Hide or Work?" *Music Ministry* 2 (October 1969):3–5, 40.

Barrows, Cliff. "Music in Evangelism." *Decision* 3 (December 1962):11–13.

_____. "Musical Evangelism." *Church Musician* 14 (October 1963):6–9.

Best, Harold. "Entertainment and Worship." *Church Music in Dimension* 2, no. 3 (1966):4–7.

_____. "There Is More to Redemption than Meets the Ear." *Christianity Today* 18 (26 July 1974):12–18.

_____. "Music: Offerings of Creativity." *Christianity Today,* May 6, 1977, pp. 12–15.

Bowes, Malcom. "Jazz in the Chapel." *Music Journal* 11 (1966):45.

Braun, H. Myron. "Mod Worship and How It Grows." *The Hymn* 22 (January 1971):48–50.

_____. "Is It Music?" *The Hymn* 23 (January 1972):14–16.

Buck, Carlton C. "What Will the Church Sing Tomorrow?" *The Hymn* 23 (January 1972):5–7.

Buddey, Anne. "Folk Hymns that 'Psych-up' Teens." *Music Journal* 6 (1967):51.

"Church Music and the Sacred-Secular Syndrome." *Church Music* 2 (1967):40.

Cleveland, Lois J. "Guitar: The 'In' Instrument." *The Hymn* 22 (January 1971):4, 6–7, 50.

Cook, Robert A. "That New Religious Music." *Christian Herald* 99 (December 1976):4–9, 65.

Curtin, Karen. "Jazzmen and Churchmen United." *Music Journal* 68 (Anthology):227.

Downey, James C. "Revivalism, the Gospel Song and Social Reform." *Ethnomusicology* 9, no. 2 (1965):115–25.

_____. "The Great Awakening and the Music of the Baptists, 1740–1800." *William Carey College Reprints* in *Faculty Bulletin* 1 (May 1970):20–27.

Elbin, Paul E. "Fanny Crosby and William H. Doane Have Had Their Day." *Music,* October 1969, pp. 42–43.

Elmer, Richard M. "Modern Evangelism and Church Music." *The Hymn* 7 (January 1956):13–17.

Eskew, Harry. "Music in the Baptist Tradition." *Review and Expositor* 69 (Spring 1972):161–75.

_____. "A Cultural Understanding of Hymnody." *The Hymn* 23 (July 1972):79–84.

Fisher, Charles M. "The Demise of Religious Music." *Music Ministry* 2 (December 1969):3–5.

Fuller, Jeanne Weaver. "What About Today's 'Style'?" *The Choral Journal* 7 (September-October 1966):10–11.

Garside, C. "Calvin's Preface to the Psalter." *Musical Quarterly* 37 (October 1951):566–77.

Gold, Carles E. "The Gospel Song: Contemporary Opinion." *The Hymn* 9 (July 1958):69–73.

Hicks, Rex. "Common Sense in Church Music." *Church Music in Dimension,* Summer 1965, pp. 2–3.

Hillard, Barbara, and Hillard, A. M. "Folk Music: Fresh Wind or Storm?" *Music Ministry* 5 (1968):6–8.

Hille, Waldemar. "Evaluating Gospel Songs." *The Hymn* 3 (January 1952):15–18.

Hillert, Richard. "Popular Church Music—Twentieth-Century Style." *Church Music* 2 (1969):1–7, 32–33, 37–38.

Holz, Richard. "Renaissance of Sacred Music in the Salvation Army." *The Hymn* 1 (April 1950):19.

Hunkins, Arthur B. "The Serious Contemporary Composer and the Church Today." *Music Ministry* 2 (February 1970):12–14.

Hustad, Donald. "Spiritual Music for a Spiritual Church." *Church Music in Dimension* 1 (Winter 1964–65):8–12.

————. "Entertainment in Evangelism." *Church Music in Dimension* 2, no. 3 (1966):1–4, 8.

————. "Music and the Church's Outreach." *Review and Expositor* 69 (Spring 1972):177–86.

Kauffman, Robert. "An Ethnomusicologist Looks at Church Music in the Seventies." *Music Ministry* 3 (December 1970):3–4.

Knight, George L. "Transient and Permanent Hymns." *The Hymn* 3 (January 1952):4, 9.

Lacour, L. "Music in Evangelism." *Music Ministry* 4 (August 1963):2.

Landgrave, Phillip. "Church Music and the 'Now Generation.'" *Review and Expositor* 59 (Spring 1972):195–98.

Lewis, C. S. "On Church Music." *English Church Music* 19 (April 1949):19–22.

Lovelace, Austin C. "Tunes Alive in '85?" *The Hymn* 23 (January 1972):8–11.

Macauley, J. C. "The Ministry of Music." *AABC Newsletter* 16 (Fall 1972):6–9.

MacCluskey, Thomas. "Rock in Its Elements." *Music Educator's Journal* 11 (1969):49–51.

Marty, Martin E. "New Patterns for a New Age." *Church Music* 2 (1967):1–4.

McElrath, Hugh. "Music in the History of the Church." *Review and Expositor* 69 (Spring 1972):141–60.

McKinney, Howard D. "Winds of Change." *Fisher Edition News* 45 (September–October 1967):2–3.

Morgan, Catherine. "The Evolution of the New." *Journal of Church Music* 7 (1970):9–10.

Morrison, John. "Toward a Philosophy of Church Music." *The Church Musician,* May 1976, pp. 47–49.

Morse, R. LaVerne. "Ethnomusicology: A New Frontier." *Evangelical Missions Quarterly* 11 (January 1975):32–37.

Newhoff, B. "America's Sacred Folk Song." *Church Musician* 14 (August 1962):10–12.

Pennington, James M. "Rock Music—Love ad infinitum, ad absurdum." *Christianity Today* 21 (8 July 1977):20–21.

Perry, C. "The Spiritual and Jazz." *International Musician* 61 (January 1963):32.

Peterson, William J. "O, What a Fantastic New Day for Christian Music." *Eternity,* April 1971, pp. 12–17.

Pfautsch, Lloyd. "I Believe; Therefore I Speak." *Music Ministry* 9 (April 1968):2–5.

_____. "Worship and Crisis in Church Music." *Music Ministry* 2 (November 1969):3–6, 40.

Pfeil, Elmer. "Catholic Music Since Vatican II: Overcoming Inertia." *The Christian Ministry* 8 (March 1977):18–19.

Pierce, Edwin H. "Gospel Hymns and Their Tunes." *The Musical Quarterly* 26 (July 1940):355–64.

Pressau, Jack R. "Emotional Reaction to Innovation in Church Music." *Music Ministry* 3 (January 1971):2–6, 42.

Reynolds, William J. "Folk Element in American Church Music." *Church Music in America* 2, no. 2 (1966):2–5.

Rice, John H., ed. "Attempts to Evangelize the Negro-slaves in Virginia and Carolina." *The Evangelical and Literary Magazine* 4 (October 1821):538–50.

Rich, Alan. "Religion with a Rock Beat." *Bravo* 11 (1972):17–19.

Ripper, Theodore W. "Finding Good in All This Mess." *Music Ministry* 5 (November 1972):8–9.

Roe, Norman D. "Dave Brubeck—Church Musician." *Music Ministry* 1 (December 1968):2–5.

Routley, Erik. "On the Billy Graham Songbook." *The Hymn* 6 (January 1955):25–28.

Schalk, Carl. "Martin Luther Is Alive and Well and Writing Acid Rock Hymns in the Wartburg." *Church Music* 2 (1969):31–32.

_____. "The New Music—Where Do We Go from Here?" *Church Music* 1 (1972):35.

_____. "Church Music in Transition: The Change in Change." *Christian Century,* December 1973, pp. 1251–6.

_____. "New Hymnals: Shaping the Future of Congregational Singing." *The Christian Ministry* 8 (March 1977):4–7.

Sims, W. H. "Music in Missions." *Church Musician* 14 (March 1963):4–10.

Smith, Emmet. "A Fairy Tale." *Sacred Music,* Spring 1969, pp. 3–11.

Stanislaw, Richard J. "Songs of the Sawdust Trail." *Eternity,* August 1976, pp. 50–51.

Summerlin, Ed. "Maybe We All Missed the Point." *Music Ministry* 2 (January 1970):7–9.

Sunderman, L. F. "Christian Upsurge through Music." *Etude* 67 (July 1949):413.

Swarm, P. "Musicians in a New Job." *Music Journal* 7 (July–August 1949):13.

Thibodeau, Ralph. "Threnody for Sacred Music, 1968, or The People of God Have Been Had." *Commonweal* 89 (13 December 1968):378–79.

Vail, James H. "Values in Church Music: A Reassessment." *The Choral Journal* 12, no. 2 (1971):9–12.

Wakefield, Gordon S. "Beliefs in Recent British Hymnody." *The Hymn* 22 (January 1971):13–19.

Winter, Miriam Therese. "The Song of Life." *Journal of Church Music,* December 1969, pp. 2–4.

Wood, D. "Jazz, Folk, Rock and the Church." *Journal of Church Music,* September 1969, p. 2.

Young, Carlton. "Pioneers of Pop Ten Years Later." *Music Ministry* 8 (May 1976):6–8.

_____. "Church Music, American Style: What's Ahead?" *The Christian Ministry* 8 (March 1977):8–11.

Zetty, Claude. "New Sounds in the Church." *The Choral Journal* 8 (May–June 1968):15–17.

Zimmermann, Heinz Werner. "And All That Jazz." *Church Music* 2 (1968):33–35.

_____. "Church Music in Pluralistic Society." *Music Ministry* 4 (March 1972):6–10.

Newspaper Articles

"Clergy Shut Out by Laymen." *Scranton Times* (Pa.), August 31, 1976.

Cornell, George. "Modern Music Featuring More Gospel Sounds." *Scranton Times* (Pa.), April 29, 1970, p. 48.

Poling, David. "Religion in America." *Scranton Times* (Pa.), March 3, 1976.

"Protestant Churches Show Renewed Interest in Evangelism." *Scranton Times* (Pa.), April 14, 1977, p. 21.

Pamphlets and Published Papers

Best, Harold. "The Climate of Creativity." *Church Music Perspectives* 1. Chicago: National Church Music Fellowship, no. 2, p. 4.

Foote, Henry Wilder. "Recent American Hymnody." Paper of the *Hymn Society of America,* no. 17, 1952.

Hustad, Donald. "Shall We Demythologize Our Hymns?" *Church Music Perspectives* 1. Chicago: National Church Music Fellowship, no. 6, p. 9.

Johansen, John Henry. "The Olney Hymns." Paper of the *Hymn Society of America,* no. 20, 1956.

Olson, Lee. "Church Music and Secularism." *Church Music Perspectives* 1. Chicago: National Church Music Fellowship, no. 4, p. 10.

Reed, Luther H. "Luther and Congregational Song." Paper of the *Hymn Society of America,* no. 12, 1947.

Rockholt, Preston. "Creative Tensions in Church Music." Paper presented at the Scholastic Honor Society Convocation, Wheaton College, Illinois, 7 March 1969.

Routley, Erik. *Is Jazz Music Christian?* London: Epworth Press, 1964. (Pamphlet.)

Lectures and Interviews

Hustad, Donald P. Music Workship of Billy Graham School of Evangelism. Lecture, New York City, 16–19 June 1969.

_____. Southern Baptist Theological Seminary, Louisville, Ky. Interview, 14 April 1977.

Landgrave, Phillip. Southern Baptist Theological Seminary, Louisville, Ky. Interview, 15 April 1977.

Unpublished Materials

Boyer, Horace Clarence. "An Analysis of Black Church Music with Examples Drawn from Services in Rochester, New York." Ph.D. dissertation, University of Rochester, Eastman School of Music, 1973.

Burnett, Madeline. "The Development of American Hymnody,

1620–1900." Master's thesis, University of Southern California, 1946.

Covey, Cyclone. "Religion and Music in Colonial America." Ph.D. dissertation, Stanford University, 1949.

Daugherty, Harold A., Jr. "A Study of John La Montaine's Trilogy of Pageant-Operas for Christmas." D.M.A. dissertation, University of Southern California, 1976.

Downey, James. "The Music of American Revivalism, 1740–1800." Ph.D. dissertation, Tulane University, 1968.

Gold, Charles E. "A Study of the Gospel Song." Master's thesis, University of Southern California, 1953.

Hall, Stephen Frederic. "The Christian Folk Musical: A Foundational Study." Master's thesis, Southern Baptist Theological Seminary, 1973.

Horner, Robert Bruce. "The Function of Music in the Youth for Christ Program." Master's thesis, Indiana University, 1970.

Hustad, Donald P. "Church Music—A Ministry for Our Time." Manuscript later published with revisions, as "Music Speaks . . . but What Language?" in *Christianity Today,* 6 May 1977.

————. "Problems in Psychology and Aesthetics in Music." Unpublished article.

Lilley, John M. "New Principles of Worship Based on Multi-Media Experience in Corporate Worship." D.M.A. dissertation, University of Southern California, 1971.

McKissick, Marvin. "A Study of the Function of Music in the Major Religious Revivals in America since 1875." Master's thesis, University of Southern California, 1957.

Meyer, Charles Huldrich Zwingli. "Sacred Lyrics of Protestant America: A Sociological Study in Compensation." Ph.D. dissertation, Northwestern University, 1933.

Quinn, Eugene F. "A Survey of the Principles and Practices of Contemporary American Non-Liturgical Church Music." D.C.M. dissertation, Southern Baptist Theological Seminary, 1963.

Renfro, Robert Chase. "A Historical Survey of Revival Music in America." Master's thesis, Southern Baptist Theological Seminary, 1950.

Ricks, George Robinson. "Some Aspects of the Religious Music of the United States Negro: An Ethnomusicological Study with Special Emphasis on the Gospel Tradition." Ph.D. dissertation, Northwestern University, 1960.

Sims, John N. "The Hymnody of the Camp-Meeting Tradition." D.S.M. dissertation, Union Theological Seminary, 1960.

Stansbury, George W. "The Music of the Billy Graham Crusades, 1947–1970: An Analysis and Evaluation." D.M.A. dissertation, Southern Baptist Theological Seminary, 1971.

Stevenson, B. Howard. "Everyman: A Creative Experiment in Church Music Drama." D.M.A. dissertation, University of Southern California, 1971.

Whitinger, Julius Edward. "Hymnody of the Early American Indian Missions." Studies in Music, no. 46. Ph.D. dissertation, Catholic University, 1971.

Williamson, Francis Hildt. "The Lord's Song and the Ministry of the Church." Doctoral dissertation, Union Theological Seminary, 1967.

Related Dissertations

Berryman, James Cleo. "Theology and Evangelism in Twentieth-Century American Protestant Christianity." Ph.D. dissertation, Southwestern Baptist Theological Seminary, 1964.

Boraine, Alexander Lionel. "The Nature of Evangelism in the Theology and Practice of John Wesley." Ph.D. dissertation, Drew University, 1969.

Brandt, Leroy D. "Socio-Geographical Influences on the Techniques of Evangelism Amongst Protestants in the United States." Ph.D. dissertation, New York University, 1937.

Brunk, George Rowland, Jr. "Some Changing Concepts in Twentieth Century Evangelism and Missiology." Ph.D. dissertation, Union Theological Seminary in Virginia, 1967.

Bush, Richard Merrell. "An Examination of the Relationship between Christian Community and Evangelism in the Local Church." D. Min. dissertation, Fuller Theological Seminary, 1975.

Carnes, Otis G. "An Effective Evangelism for the Town and Country Church." Ph.D. dissertation, Boston University School of Theology, 1952.

Cook, Clyde. "Cross-Cultural Persuasive Evangelism." D. Miss. dissertation, Fuller Theological Seminary, 1974.

Crume, Thomas Clinton. "Evangelism in Its Doctrinal and Practical Aspects." Ph.D. dissertation, The Southern Baptist Theological Seminary, 1924.

Eckenroth, Melvin K. "Principles and Methodologies of Christian Evangelism: A Study of Basic Concepts of Some Evangelical Christians in Contemporary Situations." D. Min. dissertation, Howard University, 1974.

Ellerbe, Marion Fred. "The Music Missionary of the Southern Baptist Convention: His Preparation and His Work." D.M.A. dissertation, The Catholic University of America, 1970.

Lacour, Lawrence Leland. "A Study of the Revival Method in America." Master's thesis, Northwestern University, 1956.

McLoughlin, William G., Jr. "Professional Evangelism: The Social Significance of Religious Revivals since 1865." Ph.D. dissertation, Harvard University, 1953.

Mikell, Alfred Miller. "The Contribution of Audio-Visuals to Evangelism in Religious Education." Ph.D. dissertation, Southwestern Baptist Theological Seminary, 1959.

Quinn, Eugene F. "A Survey of the Principles and Practices of Contemporary American Nonliturgical Church Music." Ph.D. dissertation, The Southern Baptist Theological Seminary, 1963.

Sheers, Charles A. "An Approach to the Theology of Evangelism." Ph.D. dissertation, Dallas Theological Seminary, 1969.

Index